Yu...a

by

DAVID ASH
with additional material by Sylvie Nickels

David Ash is a specialist in East European matters and is the author of *Essential Bulgaria* in this series.
Following 13 years as travel editor of the Daily Express, he has written freelance for a variety of national publications, including Country Life and the Daily Telegraph.

AA

Produced by the Publishing Division of
The Automobile Association

Written by David Ash with additional material by Sylvie Nickels
Peace and Quiet section
by Paul Sterry
Consultant: Frank Dawes

Edited, designed and produced by the Publishing Division of The Automobile Association. Maps © The Automobile Association 1991.

Distributed in the United Kingdom by the Automobile Association, Fanum House, Basingstoke, Hampshire, RG21 2EA

The contents of this publication are believed correct at the time of printing. Nevertheless, the publishers cannot accept responsibility for errors or omissions, nor for changes in details given. We have tried to ensure accuracy in this guide, but things do change and we would be grateful if readers could advise us of any inaccuracies they may encounter.

© The Automobile Association 1991

All rights reserved. No part of this publication may be reproduced, stored in a retrieval system, or transmitted in any form or by any means – electronic, photocopying, recording, or otherwise – unless the written permission of the publishers has been obtained beforehand.

A CIP catalogue record for this book is available from the British Library.

ISBN 0 7495 0098 0

Published by The Automobile Association

Typesetting: Microset Graphics Ltd, Basingstoke
Colour separation: L.C. Repro, Aldermaston
Printed in Italy by Printers S.R.L., Trento

Front cover picture: The Old Bridge at Mostar

CONTENTS

INTRODUCTION	4	CULTURE, ENTERTAINMENT AND NIGHTLIFE	100
BACKGROUND	7	WEATHER AND WHEN TO GO	101
BEOGRAD AND CENTRAL YUGOSLAVIA	11	HOW TO BE A LOCAL	102
THE ADRIATIC COAST AND ISLANDS	29	PERSONAL PRIORITIES	103
THE NORTH	67	CHILDREN	104
THE SOUTH	77	TIGHT BUDGET	104
PEACE AND QUIET Yugoslavia's Wildlife and Countryside	87	SPECIAL EVENTS	105
		SPORT	106
FOOD AND DRINK	97	DIRECTORY	109
SHOPPING	98	LANGUAGE	124
ACCOMMODATION	99	INDEX	127

This book employs a simple rating system to help choose which places to visit:

◆◆◆   do not miss

◆◆   see if you can

◆   worth seeing if you have time

INTRODUCTION

For the vast majority of its visitors, Yugoslavia means the Adriatic coast, with perhaps a brief foray or two inland. It is indeed, along with its several hundred islands, a magnificent coast; but it represents only a fraction of what is scenically, culturally, historically and ethnically, on offer in this, perhaps the most diverse of European countries. It would be hard, for example, to find a greater contrast than between the Alpine pastures, chalets and onion-domed churches of Slovenia in the north, and the sun-scorched ranges, multi-domed medieval Orthodox monasteries and slim minarets of Islam in the distant south of Macedonia.

These are merely visual manifestations of a land divided for centuries, only emerging within (more or less) its present boundaries in 1918. Such divisions have equally left their influences on customs, culture, food, dress – and attitudes. Thus from the point of view of you, the tourist, the service is slicker, the amenities better

INTRODUCTION

Glorious mountain scenery around Kranjska Gora in north Yugoslavia

organised, the plumbing less likely to be erratic in the north and west; but, generally speaking, the prices become lower, the markets more colourful, the villages and their way of life more intriguingly unfamiliar as you progress inland or south.

Along the coast, if you want something more than the traditional pleasures of sea and sun – albeit in a usually startlingly beautiful setting – choose your resort with care. Some provide modern complexes with every imaginable amenity, but leave you curiously isolated from the 'real' Yugoslavia. So make sure you are within strolling distance of the sort of shops, restaurants, streets, which form part of daily life for the Yugoslavs themselves. Likewise, sightseeing excursions with well-informed guides may provide the quickest and easiest way of seeing the major sights, but local buses or boats will stop in communities where most visitors do not go and give opportunities to meet the Yugoslavs – who are eminently 'meetable' – in a way you certainly will not if you stick to the packaged arrangement.

INTRODUCTION

Whether you are touring or exploring from a fixed base, it is well worth every moment of advance planning to make sure you do not miss those mountains, monasteries, mosques, museums or markets, most likely to catch the essence of Yugoslavia for you personally.
If you possibly can, avoid the peak months of July and August, when the coast is jammed with tourists, the prices are at their highest, and the temperatures too. May and October can be particularly lovely, prices are much lower, and there is elbow room to spare.

Most visitors stay on the coast or islands... and with places as pretty as Hvar, no wonder!

BACKGROUND

Yugoslavia is made up of six republics: Bosnia-Hercegovina (Bosna i Hercegovina) in the centre; Croatia (Hrvatska), north and coast; Macedonia (Makedonija) in the far south; Montenegro (Crna Gora) in the southwest; Serbia (Serbija), including the autonomous regions of Kosovo and Vojvodina, in the east; and Slovenia (Slovenija) in the north. Yugoslavia means 'Land of the South Slavs', but long before the Slavs arrived on the scene its territory had seen the coming and going of ancient civilisations – the traces of some even now still being uncovered. For centuries, the Romans made it part of their empire and, before they left, it was already divided: the north and west falling into the Latin and Catholic world, the south and east absorbed by the Orthodoxy of Byzantium, in due course adopting the Cyrillic alphabet.

In the wake of various barbarian invasions, the Slavs arrived in about the 6th century. By the 12th century, the Serbs were establishing their own medieval empire, creating monasteries with luminous frescos, many of which marvellously survive. But their sway was short-lived. During the 14th century, the Ottoman Turks spilled into Europe, from the late part of that century occupying 'Byzantine' areas of Yugoslavia on their way to the gates of Vienna. Their rule lasted over 500 years. Slovenia and inland Croatia, in the meantime, were drawn into the Habsburg fold, while coastal Istria (Istra) and Dalmatia (Dalmacija), to varying degrees and for varying periods, alternated between local rulers and the Venetians, the latter leaving their mark on the architecture of island and coastal communities. Serbia was the first to throw off Turkish rule in the 19th century; the Balkan Wars of 1912-13 finally ended it in more southerly regions. And, at last, World War I changed the entire face of Europe, spawning new independent nations from the shattered Austro-Hungarian empire, among them what became the Kingdom of Yugoslavia. Alas, it was bedevilled by nationalist conflict, notably between the Serbs and Croats, the former seeking a kind of

Folk music and dance are very much alive – and not simply to entertain visitors

BACKGROUND

BACKGROUND

YUGOSLAVIA

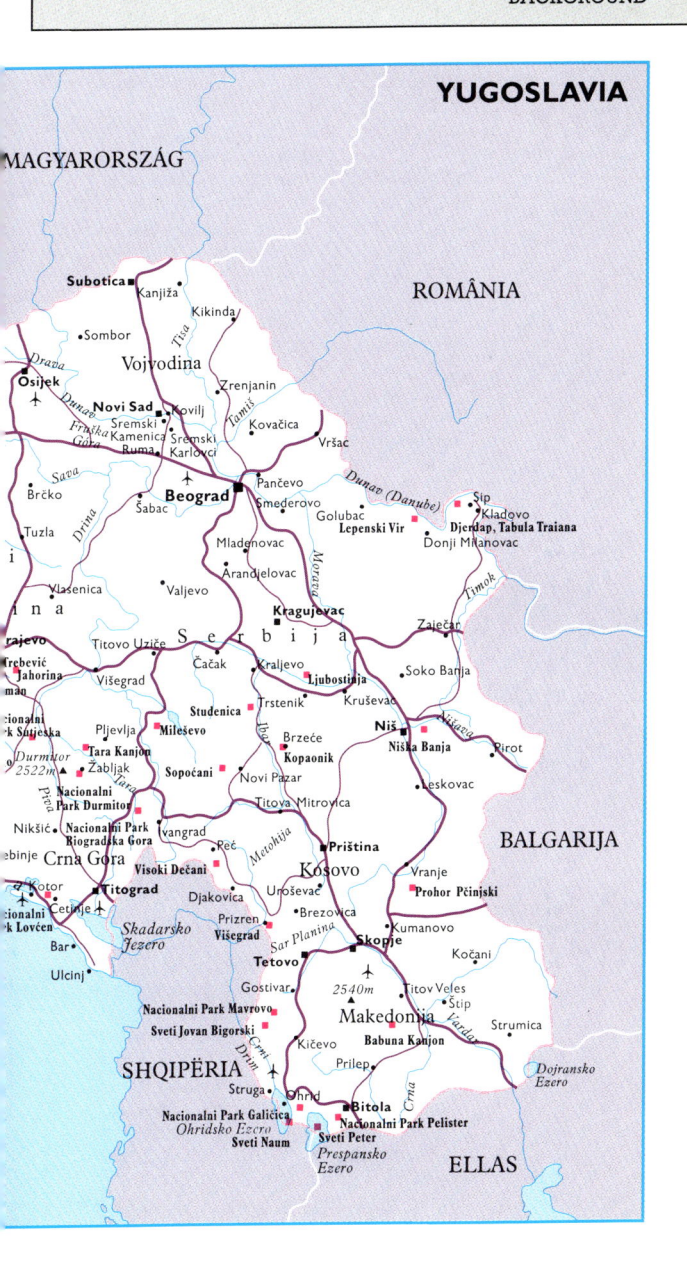

BACKGROUND

'greater Serbia', the latter wanting autonomy for each region.

The conflict unhappily continued into World War II, intensified by the development of the pro-Nazi Ustaše movement of Croatia. But finally, out of the devastation, the majority of Yugoslavs found common cause against the real enemy under the leadership of Josip Brož Tito and his Partisans. By the end of the war, 1.75 million Yugoslavs were dead, the country's communications and industries shattered, but a new sense of unity had emerged and a fierce willingness to rebuild. Tito was no angel, but he gave the new nation the leadership it needed, as well as a fierce sense of independence, resulting in a break from Stalinist influences in 1948. Under Tito, the rights of Yugoslavia's many non-Slav nationalities – Hungarians and Albanians being the largest of a dozen or so 'minorities' – were guaranteed. The system of workers' self-management (as opposed to State control) was firmly established, private enterprise, in a small way, was allowed to flourish – and tourism boomed.

But under the surface, economically all was far from well. Over-spending and under-production ultimately resulted in mega-inflation, growing unemployment and increasing dissatisfaction. And, following Tito's death in 1980, the system of a rotating presidency which he bequeathed to the country, left a power vacuum which has yet to be filled. Nationalism has once again reared its head, leading to bloody conflict between Serb and Albanian in the autonomous region of Kosovo in south Serbia, and reviving old grudges between Serb and Croat.

As this book goes to press and Yugoslavia edges into a market economy, enormous achievements have been made in combating inflation, hopefully forecast as 25 per cent for 1991 (compared with 3,000 per cent in 1989!); new winds of democracy have blown non-Communists into power in Slovenia and Croatia. And a revised Constitution promises new solutions for old problems. With a country of six such diverse republics, peopled by 23.5 million individualists, Yugoslavia's friends can only watch and hope.

BEOGRAD

The National Museum in Beograd, an imposing home for fine exhibits

BEOGRAD AND CENTRAL YUGOSLAVIA

Relatively few foreign visitors penetrate the mountains backing Yugoslavia's Adriatic coastal strip, to explore the country's heartland and capital. Yet the broad swath of country from the Dinaric mountain chain in the west to the Danube gorges in the east includes spectacular scenery and historic cities such as Beograd and Sarajevo.

BEOGRAD (BELGRADE)

Beograd actually means 'White City'. While not as beautiful as Prague or Budapest, it has among its charms plenty of indigenous elegance which survived the 1941 bombing, international modern hotels exuding Western-style sophistication, well-equipped congress centres, a highly enjoyable river embankment, and a warm humanity permeating areas such as Skadarlija, 'bohemian'.

Set on slight eminences by the Dunav (Danube) – and its confluence with the Sava river – Beograd is capital of the Serbian Republic as well as of federal Yugoslavia.
Although Croatian-born, Marshal Tito, the Father of modern Yugoslavia, declared: 'I loved Beograd always, and I always longed to come to Beograd as soon as possible. It was a feeling like when a man wants to see his birthplace after long years of absence.'
His wish was to be buried there, in his 'Flower House' villa on a tree-guarded hill (see page 13). Beograd has 40 museums and galleries, an opera-house, ballet, ten theatres, four concert halls, four symphony orchestras, choral groups, professional folk dance ensembles, amateur drama, music, and other art societies. Stars of rock and pop music are frequent guests of Beograd.

BEOGRAD

History
The city's site, between two great rivers, has been occupied for over 7,000 years. Early settlers were followed by Celts and then the Romans, who in the 1st century AD took over the Celtic town to establish a city, Singidunum, with a typical grid pattern of streets.
At the end of the Roman Empire, the city, being at the frontier of eastern and western powers, suffered repeated attacks, but came under Byzantine rule in 488. It was finally conquered by the Slavs and became the 'White City' (Beli Grad).
From the 9th to 16th centuries, Beograd fell at different times into the hands of Franks, Bulgars, Magyars, Crusaders, Serbs and Ottoman Turks. It flourished for a while as an oriental city in the 17th century, but its possession was once again violently disputed – this time by Austrians and Turks – throughout the 18th century. The 19th century saw more mayhem, with massacres, Serbian uprisings and renewed Turkish depredations. The Turks did not finally depart until 1867.
Beograd suffered again during the two World Wars, but it became the capital of the new kingdom of the Serbs, Croats and Slovenes in 1918 and eventually the federal capital. The city has grown since the end of World War II. It now has a population of close on 1.5 million and a whole new district, Novi (New) Beograd, on the left bank of the River Sava.

What to See

◆
BAJRAKLI DŽAMIJA (BAJRAKLI MOSQUE)
Ulica Gospodar Jevremova 11
Beograd's only surviving mosque dates from 1690. Its name means 'Flag Mosque', a reference to the flag it used to fly to indicate the hour of prayer to the other city mosques. It was, for a time in the 18th century, a Christian church. To enter the mosque, visitors descend a flight of steps to a level below the present street.

◆◆
GALERIJA FRESAKA (FRESCO GALLERY)
Ulica Cara Uroša 20
The museum is of particular interest to enthusiasts for Byzantine art. It contains around 800 copies of medieval wall paintings from the most important churches and monasteries of Serbia, Macedonia, Montenegro and Bosnia-Hercegovina.
Open: Tuesday, Wednesday and Friday 10.00-17.00 hrs; Thursday 10.00-19.00 hrs; Saturday 09.00-17.00 hrs; Sunday 10.00-14.00 hrs. *Closed:* Monday.

◆
JOSIP BROŽ TITO SPOMENIK (TITO MEMORIAL CENTRE)
The memorial centre is in a park just south of the city centre, in the residential district of Dedinje. The main entrance is on Bulevar Oktobarske Revolucije. It can be reached by bus from Trg Republike. Sculptures adorn the park and the complex includes Tito's Residence, the Flower House

BEOGRAD

(its winter garden), the Billiard (hobby) House, Hunting House, 'Old' Museum, 25 May Museum, 4 July Museum, and a new building with a further memorial collection, all illustrating various aspects of Tito's life and times. In **Tito's Mausoleum**, his flower-flanked gravestone is inscribed with his name and years of birth and death only. The constant Guard of Honour, four blue-uniformed members of the Yugoslav People's Army, is changed every 15 minutes. *Open:* daily 09.00-16.00 hrs.

♦♦♦
KALEMEGDAN
northeast part of the city
Beograd's great fortress of Kalemegdan is set in a fine park. The name is Turkish, meaning 'town field'.
The Celts first built a fort on the hill near the confluence of the Danube and Sava Rivers, and the Romans enlarged it. Nothing of the Celtic and little of the Roman structures remains. Most of the visible fortifications are much later – Turkish or Austrian. The fortress has an upper ward, with moat, and a lower ward. Look out, in the upper ward for splendid **views** of the Danube and Sava, the 18th-century **clock tower**, the 15th-century tower now housing an **observatory**, the **Ružica church** with wall paintings, and the 43-foot (13m) **column** topped by the *Messenger of Victory* by Yugoslavia's best known sculptor, Ivan Meštrović. In the lower ward, note **Prince**

Beograd's Kalemegdan fortress

BEOGRAD

Eugene's Gate, commemorating Austria's victory over the Turks in 1717 and the infamous prison called the **Nebojša Tower**, down by the Danube.
The surrounding park contains sculptures, the **Cvijeta Zuzporić Art Pavilion** (putting on regular exhibitions), and **Beograd Zoo**.
The **Vojni Muzej** (Military Museum), also in Kalemegdan park, encapsulates Yugoslavia's violent history of occupation and resistance with vivid displays.
Museum open: daily (except Monday) 10.00-17.00 hrs.

◆
KONAK KNEGINJE LJUBICE (PRINCESS LJUBICE'S MANSION)
Kneza Sime Markovića 3
Kneginje (Princess) Ljubice, who gives her name to this typical upper-class Balkan house of the 19th century, was the jealous wife of the Serbian leader Prince Miloš Obrenović. The mansion was built in 1829-31; its façade was restored in 1978. Inside are the typical furnishings of a well-to-do family of the time (not actually those of the princess), combining Oriental and Western elements.
Open: Tuesday, Thursday and Friday 10.00-17.00hrs; Wednesday 12.00-19.00 hrs; Saturday and Sunday 09.00-16.00 hrs. *Closed:* Monday

◆
MUZEJ SAVREMENE UMETNOSTI (MUSEUM OF CONTEMPORARY ART)
Ušće Save 66, Novi Beograd
The museum is a 1960s building housing a large collection of 20th-century Yugoslav art – drawings, paintings, sculpture. The aims of the museum are largely educational and the works of art are well displayed, if not of great overall artistic significance.
Open: Monday and Wednesday to Friday 12.00-19.00 hrs; Saturday and Sunday 10.00-17.00hrs. *Closed:* Tuesday. Reached by Bus 16 or 36 from the steps below Brankova.

◆◆◆
NARODNI MUZEJ (NATIONAL MUSEUM)
Trg Republike
The National Museum, founded in 1844 and housed in its present building since 1946, has exceptional prestige, with valuable collections of prehistoric, ancient and medieval archaeology, frescos, and more recent Serbian art. Look out, in the classical section, for the gold masks from Trebenište, Greek gold jewellery from Ohrid and Roman sculptures, including a bronze head of the locally-born (in Niš) Roman Emperor Constantine the Great. Medieval items – notably frescos and icons – are on the first floor; Yugoslav and European art from the 15th to 20th centuries on the top floor.
Open: Tuesday, Wednesday and Friday 10.00-17.00 hrs; Thursday 10.00-19.00 hrs; Saturday 09.00-17.00 hrs; Sunday 10.00-14.00 hrs. *Closed:* Monday.

◆◆
SKADARLIJA
off Trg Republike
Skadarlija is an attractively conserved topographical scrapbook of Bohemian old Beograd, an echo of Soho or

BEOGRAD

Greenwich Village – but without seediness or pornography. Actors, poets and painters are said to haunt the café tables on the cobbles of its sloping streets, and student discussion puts the world to rights, while (as in other Yugoslav tourist enclaves) a quick-sketch artist may record the visitor's likeness quite commendably at the price.

Excursions

◆◆
AVALA

This is a wooded hill in a fine setting 12 miles (20km) to the south of the city, crowned by the Monument to an Unknown Soldier, the work of Yugoslavia's best known sculptor, Ivan Meštrović.

IRON GATE GORGE see page 19

Accommodation

Beograd has a good selection of hotels, particularly in the more expensive ranges.

Beograd Inter-Continental, Vladimira Popovića 10 (tel: (011) 138-708). Glamorous scene and politely efficient service – sometimes with a smile. 577 beds. De luxe category.

Jugoslavija, Bulevar Eduarda Kardelja 3, Zemun (tel: (011) 600-222). Entertainment available includes a casino and night-club. 460 rooms. De luxe category.

Metropol, Bulevar Revolucije (tel: (011) 330-911). On one of the main boulevards, but surrounded on three sides by Tašmajdan Park. 224 rooms. A category.

Srbija, Ustanička 127c (tel: (011) 489-04-04). Modern tower block hotel with 331 rooms. B category.

Šumadija, Šumadijski Trg 8 (tel: (011) 554-255). Near the sports centre, the Beograd Fair (indoor and outdoor exhibition areas) and the racecourse. 101 rooms. B category.

Trim, Kneza Višeslava 72 (tel: (011) 558-128). A small hotel (41 rooms) but with its own restaurant/café. C category.

Turist, Sarajevska 37 (tel: (011) 682-855). Near the railway station and Beograd Fair. 89 rooms. B category.

Entertainment and Nightlife

Beograd revels in culture, the arts, festivals and fairs, including (with fringe fun) the FEST – Best World Films (February); BITEF (Beograd International Theatre Festival), a review of world avant-garde theatrical trends (September); BEMUS – Beograd Musical Festival presenting serious music, opera and ballet with well-known foreign artists (October); and the Beograd Jazz Festival (November).

The city has a lively nightlife, with cafés, restaurants, night-clubs, and casinos, including one at the Metropol Hotel.

Eating Out

Restaurants with al fresco terraces offer excellent regional or international fare at prices far below the rip-off rate of some capital cities. Waiters may wear dashing Serbian gear. Folk musicians tend to leer ingratiatingly at diners, violin bows almost combing the odd coiffure as they swoop through gypsy lament, schmaltz, or perceived 'national' tune. (As elsewhere in eastern Europe,

BEOGRAD

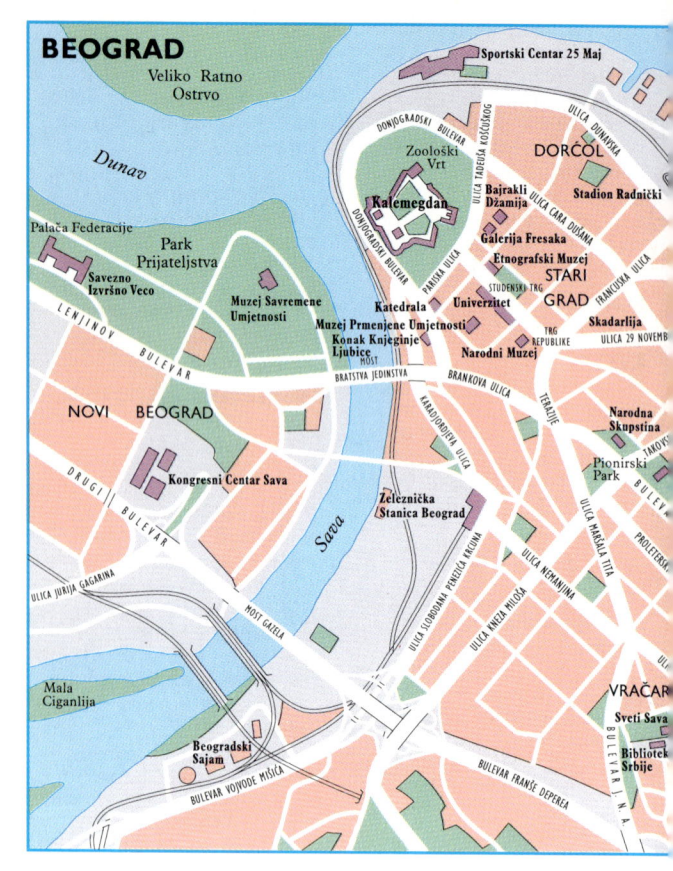

BEOGRAD
Veliko Ratno
Ostrvo

Dunav

Sportski Centar 25 Maj
DONJOGRADSKI BULEVAR
ULICA TADEUŠA KOŠĆUŠKOG
ULICA DUNAVSKA
Zoološki Vrt
DORĆOL
Bajrakli Džamija
ULICA CARA DUŠANA
Stadion Radnički
Kalemegdan
Palača Federacije
Park Prijateljstva
Galerija Fresaka
Etnografski Muzej
STUDENTSKI TRG
STARI GRAD
Savezno Izvršno Veco
PARISKA ULICA
FRANCUSKA ULICA
Muzej Savremene Umjetnosti
Katedrala
Univerzitet
LENJINOV BULEVAR
Muzej Prmenjene Umjetnosti
Konak Knjeginje Ljubice
MOST
Narodni Muzej
TRG REPUBLIKE
Skadarlija
ULICA 29 NOVEMB
BRATSTVA JEDINSTVA
BRANKOVA ULICA
NOVI BEOGRAD
KARAĐORĐEVA ULICA
TERAZIJE
Narodna Skupstina
TAKOVS
Pionirski Park
DRUGI BULEVAR
Kongresni Centar Sava
BULEVAR
Železnička Stanica Beograd
Sava
ULICA MARŠALA TITA
PROLETERSKA
ULICA JURIJA GAGARINA
ULICA SLOBODANA PENEZIĆA KRCUNA
ULICA NEMANJINA
MOST GAZELA
ULICA KNEZA MILOŠA
VRAČAR
Mala Ciganlija
Sveti Sava
Biblioteka Srbije
Beogradski Sajam
BULEVAR VOJVODE MIŠIĆA
BULEVAR FRANŠE DEPEREA

the all-purpose British air is often *My Bonny Lies Over the Ocean.*)

The Museum of Contemporary Art (see page 14) offers handy browsing for anyone who has lunched aboard one of the converted barque restaurants (fish specialities) on the River Sava, watching passing barges and a fisherman in a scull who attracts catch with a sonic echo device.

One of Beograd's plushest restaurants is that of the **Hotel Moskva,** Balkanska 1 (tel: (011) 686-255) – full of *fin-de-siècle* elegance with its own string quartet. There are many less expensive restaurants – the **Proleće** in Vuk Karadžiča, offers a good and not too expensive selection of Serbian dishes. The **London Restaurant,** on the corner of Ulica Maršal Tita and Ulica Kneza Miloša, has a

BEOGRAD/CENTRAL YUGOSLAVIA

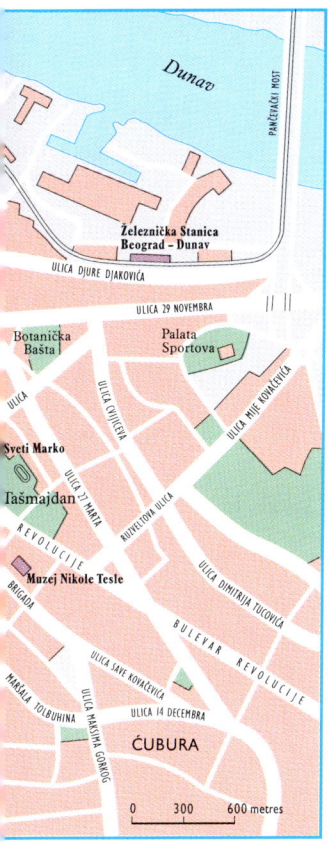

Shopping
Ulica Kneza Miloša is Beograd's shopping and commercial centre. Laid out in 1842, it is the oldest and one of the most attractive streets in the city. Around here broad streets are pleasantly pedestrianised (others being subject to double-parked vehicles, with apparently less harassment from uniformed officials than drivers encounter in Western cities). Here, you will find shops, boutiques, department stores, bookstores, antique shops and art galleries, open until well into the evening.

Of several lively open air markets, the main one is at Zeleni Venac in the centre (open seven days a week). A bargain-buying binge might take in leather and fur products, fashionable dresses and suits, embroidered blouses and dresses, Yugoslav lace, unique silver filigree jewellery, wool carpets from Pirot and Ivanjica in Serbia, camping and sports equipment, hunting and fishing tackle. Icons, works by naïve painters and sculptors, silver, gold, ceramics, and glass ornaments might be among your souvenirs.

self-service restaurant with international dishes and typical Slav food.

Skadarlija's several restaurants serve traditional Serbian food in a romantic setting. There is usually seating in the garden as well as indoors.

If you just want a snack try Skadarlija's cafés or the 'stand-up' eateries behind the railway station, which sell local 'fast food'.

WHAT TO SEE IN CENTRAL YUGOSLAVIA

◆
BANJA KANJÏZA (KANJIŽA SPA)
Vojvodina

Sufferers from chronic low back pain come for a week or more of treatment at the **Kanjiža Spa hotel and therapy centre,** near Subotica, and it is claimed that 80 per cent of them go home to

CENTRAL YUGOSLAVIA

enjoy considerable relief from this common but stubborn affliction for at least a year. Success is also recorded with patients – they are called guests – with rheumatic or skin conditions.

Treatments variously include electrophysiology, sonic therapy, acupuncture, hydro-galvanic baths, underwater high-pressure bubble massage, and gentle exercise in a gymnasium and/or the therapeutic pools of the spa's thermal (cooled to 18°C/65°F) mineral water containing sodium bicarbonate sulphide – biologically active, like the mud which is also used. The centre's purpose-built premises are set in a mature park, with sophisticated hotel and sports facilities, SKY satellite TV reception, and more than 250 employees (including medical staff).

Sports personalities use Kanjiža for pre-competitive toning up, as well as for treatment of injuries. They can relax with fishing, or make a cross-border outing to Budapest.

Near a rare gingko tree in the centre's garden is a small statue of the gipsy girl who is said to have discovered the 'miraculous' local springwater when it cured her foot ailment.

Information: Centar za rehabilitaciju i rekreaciju 'Banja', 24420 Kanjiža (tel: (024) 871-524, 871-826).

◆
BANJA LUKA
Bosnia-Hercegovina
The Romans established a spa here when they found the sulphur springs near by at Gornji Šeher. Their military station was the site of a later (14th-century) castle, but the town had its heyday under the Turks, who captured it in 1528 and even made it, for a time, the seat of the Supreme Bey. In the present century, Banja Luka attained fame as a headquarters of the Resistance. A huge war memorial on Šehetluci hill outside the town is a reminder of those days.

The town was severely damaged in an earthquake in 1969, and this has resulted in a spate of undistinguished modern building. However, some remnants of the old Bosnian town, with its Turkish flavour, can still be seen.

Ferhadija Džamija (Ferhad Pasha Mosque), built in 1583, has been restored after war and earthquake damage. It is a fine example of Islamic architecture, graceful from the outside and vividly decorated inside.

There are other examples of Turkish-Bosnian buildings in the older section of town on the left bank of the River Vrbas. Little remains of the castle on the river bank. The site now contains the **Muzej Bosanske Krajine** which consists of an ethnographical museum and a Resistance museum.

Open: Tuesday to Friday 09.00-13.00 and 17.00-19.00 hrs; Saturday and Sunday 09.00-13.00 hrs. *Closed:* Monday.

Accommodation
This includes the A category **Bosna** hotel (tel: (078) 41-355) which has 344 beds; and the **Motel International** (tel: (078) 32-777) with 120 beds.

CENTRAL YUGOSLAVIA

Guarding the river: Golubački Grad

♦♦♦ DJERDAP (IRON GATE) GORGE

Iron Gate Gorge, on Yugoslavia's border with Romania, is the most attractive part of the whole course of the Dunav (Danube) in Yugoslavia – the area is protected as a National Park from Golubac to Sip. The whole length of this stretch of the river is 60 miles (100km), the longest gorge in Europe. It is composed of four sections: Gornja, Gospodjin Vir, Big and Small Kazan and Sip gorges.

The appearance of Iron Gate Gorge was changed enormously by the building of the Djerdap dam and power plant, a joint Yugoslav-Romanian project completed in 1972, virtually turning the Danube into a narrow twisting lake. The power plant can be visited on the Yugoslav side (produce your passport and do not take photographs).

On the Yugoslav side there are steep mountains, forests, and clusters of small whitewashed houses. The Romanian side is similar but with fewer communities.

A popular excursion from Beograd is by hydrofoil down the Danube to the Iron Gate (Djerdap). The trip takes in: **Smederevo** (not in the gorge itself). The town of Smederevo was first mentioned in 1381, but gained importance after the battle of Kosovo in 1389 (the defeat of the Serbians by the Turks), when the last ruler of Serbia, Prince Branković, decided to make it his capital and to fortify it against the ever-advancing Turks with the spectacular triangular fortress (1428 to 1430) on the confluence with the River Jezava. The walls are 14½ feet (4.5m) thick and 1,640 feet (500m) long, the 19 towers are up to 82 feet (25m) in height, and there are five gates. There are no interior buildings due to bombing and a huge ammunition explosion in World War II. The rest of Smederevo is mainly industrial and uninteresting.

Golubac, at the mouth of the

CENTRAL YUGOSLAVIA

gorge, is a cosy little town with an impressive ruined fortress 2½ miles (4km) downstream. **Golubački Grad** fortress is one of the most beautiful and best preserved monuments of medieval military architecture in Serbia.

It was built above the river by the Hungarians in 1337 to guard the entrance to the first gorge. On the highest and most inaccessible bluff stands 'hat-tower'; eight more towers stand in two rows in a fan-like arrangement towards the west. On the bank of the river there is a low octagonal cannon harbour. A modern road passes through the fortress, which somehow adds to its attraction. Unfortunately, there is a quarry close by.

Accommodation: Hotel Golubački Grad (tel: (012) 88-207), 100 beds. B category.

Lepenski Vir, reached by bus from Donji Milanovac (see below), is the most important prehistoric site in Yugoslavia, with traces of civilisation dating back to 6000 BC. Settlement lasted some 2,000 years and finds have shown no resemblance to anything else unearthed in Europe from that period. Archaeologists found 70 houses and magnificent sculptures, mostly life-sized, human heads. The function of the settlement is still subject to discussion, since graves were found in the houses. The original site is now flooded; the finds were transferred to a higher plateau and there is a small museum (some objects can be seen in the National Museum in Beograd). This site should not be missed.

Donji Milanovac is a pleasant little town known as the 'town of roses'. It seems that the microclimate in this part of the artificial lake is perfect for growing flowers, especially roses, and houses are filled with them. The town is quite new, replacing the original village of the same name submerged when the dam was built.

Accommodation: Hotel Lepenski Vir (tel: (030) 86-131) is A category and has 465 beds.

Continuing down the gorge, at its narrowest point **Trajan's Tablet** (Tabula Traiana) can be seen carved into the rock. It commemorates the completion of the military road by the emperor Trajan in the 2nd century AD – an astonishing feat unfortunately now invisible below the raised waters.

Kladovo lies a few miles beyond the dam. A little beyond it are impressive traces of the bridge built by Trajan in AD103-105.

Accommodation: Hotel Djerdap (tel: (019) 88-770), 330 beds, B category.

General Information: Nacionalni Park Djerdap, 19220 Donji Milanovac, M Tita 14 (tel: (030) 86-788).

◆◆
FRUŠKA GORA
Vojvodina
The wooded hills of Fruška Gora form the only National Park in the Vojvodina autonomous region. It is famous for its wines. A popular picnic and excursion destination for

CENTRAL YUGOSLAVIA

the local people of the surrounding towns, Fruška Gora is also splendid for walkers and for monastery buffs. Several monasteries date from the 16th to 18th centuries when Serbs from further south moved here to escape from Turkish oppression.

The most important or attractive of the 20 or so monasteries are: **Krusedol,** five miles (8km) from the village of Irig. Dating from the early 16th century, it was much altered in the 18th century. The monastery complex with its church is in a particularly harmonious setting. Look for the freemasonry sign on the grave of the fourth patriarch in the church.

Vrdnik, 4½ miles (7km) from Irig, was first mentioned in 1589. It has also been known as Ravanica since the body of the revered Serbian leader Tsar Lazar was transferred here, for safety, from Ravanica monastery, nearly 100 miles (160km) to the south, in 1683.

Novo Hopovo, two miles (3km) from Iriški Venac (the main destination for excursions to the Fruška Gora), has the most monumental architecture of all the monasteries. The frescos in the church include some showing the influence of painters from Mount Athos in Greece.

Accommodation

There is little on offer. You could try the **Hotel Banja Termal** in Vrdnik, which has a swimming pool filled with mineral water. Tel: (022) 465-429. 265 beds. B category.
General Information: Nacionalni Park Fruška Gora, 21208 Sremska Kamenika, Zmajev Trg 1 (tel: (021) 616-306 and 614-650).

◆◆
JAJCE
Bosnia-Hercegovina
The town is the birthplace of the Socialist Republic of Yugoslavia, as the new federal state was proclaimed here in November

White water at Jajce

CENTRAL YUGOSLAVIA

1943 by the Anti-Fascist Council for the National Liberation of Yugoslavia, and Josip Brož (Tito) appointed Marshal. Its history, which goes back to Roman times, also includes a spell, in the 15th century, as capital of the kings of Bosnia. It was held by the Hungarians from 1464 to 1526, then fell to the Turks without resistance, most of the inhabitants having already embraced Islam. Thereafter the town flourished.

Jajce's best known sight is the much-photographed waterfall, where the River Pliva cascades 100 feet (30m) to join the River Vrbas below. However, these days it is not so easy to view the falls, and a nearby steelworks does not add to the charm of the scene.

The old town is still of considerable interest. The **castle,** now a ruin, was built in the 14th century by Hrvoke Vukčić, forebear of the Bosnian kings. It stands on a hill above the streets of the old town with their characteristic Turkish-Bosnian buildings.

The **Catacombs,** also built by Vukčić, are in a crypt or underground church. Although never finished, they contain Vukčić's grave and bear his coat of arms over the entrance. There are carved symbols on the walls which suggest Bogomil connections (the Bogomils were members of a mysterious religious sect, active in the Balkans from the 10th to the 16th centuries). To view the Catacombs, you must have a guide from the Tourist Bureau (see page 23).

Mithraic Shrine. Roman soldiers carried the cult of Mithras to many parts of the empire. This underground shrine was built within the Roman fortress. It contains a typical Mithraic relief of the god sacrificing a bull. A Tourist Bureau guide is needed to visit the shrine.

The campanile is about all that remains of the church of **Sveti Luka** (St Luke). The relics of the saint were once held here – they are now in St Mark's in Venice.

The **Museum of the National Struggle for Liberation,** housed in the hall where the federal state was proclaimed, is probably more popular with locals than with foreign visitors. *Open:* daily 08.00-12.00 and 13.00-19.00 hrs.

Accommodation

In category A, there is the **Jajce** (tel: (070) 33-285), which has 155 beds. The **Turist** (tel: (070) 33-268) has 82 beds and is category B. The **Plivska Jezera (tel: (070) 34-284), with 62 beds, is category C. All have restaurants.**

The pilgrimage town of Medjugorje receives thousands of visitors

CENTRAL YUGOSLAVIA

In Mostar, souvenir shops cram the streets where craftsmen once worked

Excursion
The Pliva Lakes, five miles (8km) west of the town make a pleasant excursion or place to stay. Old wooden watermills can be seen beside the road between Jajce and the lakes.

Turist Biro, Ulica Maršala Tito (tel: (070) 21-630).

◆
MEDJUGORJE
Bosnia-Hercegovina
On 24 June 1981, a vision of the Blessed Virgin Mary first appeared to a group of six children in this remote mountain village, with predictions of world-changing events to be kept secret by the children until some appropriate time. Eleven million pilgrims from all over the world have visited Medjugorje in the nine years since. It is constantly crowded and constantly growing.
Medjugorje (meaning 'among the hills') is about an hour's drive from the Adriatic along narrow roads, southwest of Mostar where grapes (producing *Žilavka* and *Blatina* wines) and tobacco are grown. A new church has been built and is always packed for the masses held every hour. A 46-foot (14m) high cross was erected on nearby Križevac hill in 1933. Near the church are shops selling souvenirs.

Accommodation
Visitors are accommodated in modern private buildings, including those of the recently built **Kompas-Apro Hotel Village Suma Grmine** (tel: (088) 650-005), a B category establishment with 300 beds. Accommodation information is available from PUTNIK, Yugoslav Travel Company, 11000 Beograd, Dragoslava Jovanovića 1 (tel: (011) 331-030, 339-080 and 333-187).

◆◆
MOSTAR
Bosnia-Hercegovina
The famous Turkish bridge makes Mostar a popular tourist excursion, but few visitors stay long in a town said to be the

CENTRAL YUGOSLAVIA

hottest in Yugoslavia in the summer.
From 1552, the Turks governed Hercegovina from Mostar, and left only in 1877. Nearly half the present population is still Muslim and the town has quite an Oriental aspect. It was a centre for handicrafts – notably metalwork – in the 16th and 17th centuries, but antiques and fine craftwork are hard to come by now among the tourist trash.
The shapely **bridge** of 1566 crosses the River Neretva in a high-arching single span. Boys dive from it into the river 65 feet (20m) below – for a fee; a diving competition is held in the summer. The **Kujundžiluk** (former goldsmiths' quarter), leading from the bridge, is lined with souvenir shops.
Two mosques worth a look are:

The entrance to Novi Sad's massive and complex Petrovaradin Fortress

Paša Koski Džamija, with its pleasant, cobbled courtyard fountain and domed 17th-century tomb. Climb the minaret for a fine view.
Karadzoz Beg Džamija, built in the 16th century and on a more grandiose scale. Its most precious possession is a 14th-century copy of the Koran.
Biščevića Kuća, Alajbegovića Kuća and **Kajtazova Kuća** are typical houses from the Turkish period with furnishings in the original style.
Open: daily 09.00-19.00 hrs during high season. Out of season, visits can be arranged.

Accommodation
Mostar's newest hotel is the A

CENTRAL YUGOSLAVIA

category **Ruža** (tel: (088) 36-526, 36-527), near the Old Bridge. 155 beds.

Excursions

The village of **Blagaj,** six miles (10km) south of Mostar, has a castle on a hill above and a restored Dervish monastery. The source of the River Buna gushes from a rock face near the monastery.

The pilgrimage centre of **Medjugorje** (see page 23) is about 21 miles (30km) to the southwest.

◆
NOVI SAD
Vojvodina

Capital of the autonomous region of Vojvodina and an important trade fair centre with arts activities, Novi Sad thrives on the left bank of the Danube, near the richly wooded Fruška Gora hills. It builds river ships, refines oil, and processes both metal and food (Vojvodina being the 'wheat basket' of Yugoslavia).

Trg Slobode, a spacious square, is the hub of the city. City centre streets are flanked by ensembles of exuberant period architecture, and are extensively pedestrianised. A large new contemporary-style complex has been greeted with mixed feelings – and its white marble-type facings have been daubed with sentiments supportive of British soccer teams, in well-spelt English.

The **Petrovaradin Fortress** ranks among the largest fortifications of its kind and has been dubbed 'The Gibraltar on the Danube'. It is situated on the river's right bank, overlooking Novi Sad. On foundations of earlier Roman, Hungarian and Turkish forts, it was built on 11 levels to the design of French military architect Marshal Sebastian Vauban (1692-1780). A complex series of underground tunnels adds to the interest. The castle's river-dominating section is now a characterful hotel, and there is a restaurant with an open-air extension on to ramparts.

The **Bishop's Palace** dominates the old city heart. The **Roman Catholic Cathedral** and the **Old City Hall** are among the most attractive buildings in the city centre. The interesting old **Synagogue** provides a striking contrast to the modern architecture of the **Serbian National Theatre.**

The **Muzej Vojvodjanski,** Dunavska 53 (tel: (021) 26-766), contains an interesting collection of ancient burial artefacts found along the Danube and Sava rivers.
Open: generally daily, except Mondays, 08.00-15.00 hrs.

The **Galerija Matice Srpske,** Trg Proleterskih Brigada 1 (tel: (021) 24-155), has works by local artists, most notably Paja Jovanović.
Open: Tuesday and Thursday 08.00-19.00 hrs; Wednesday, Friday and Saturday 08.00-15.00 hrs; Sunday 09.00-13.00 hrs.
Closed: Mondays.

Accommodation

There are six hotels (all B category) within the 'Varadin' organisation, two of which are **Hotel Vojvodina** (tel: (021) 622-122) with 130 beds and **Hotel Tvrdjava Varadin** (tel: (021) 431-122), 81 beds.

CENTRAL YUGOSLAVIA

Culture and Entertainment
Novi Sad is a literary city, with many publishing houses, the Writers' Community, and TV and radio stations which broadcast in the five languages of the different nationalities of Vojvodina (Serbo-Croat, Hungarian, Romanian, Ruthenian and Slovak). Popular cultural and art events include the **Yugoslav Theatre Festival** and **Poetry and Art Festival.** At **Dunavska,** the city's most popular meeting area, there are free concerts, film shows and folk performances on summer evenings.
The large Novi Sad Fair site annually services four international fairs. There is also the 'Vojvodina' Sports and Business Centre in the centre of Novi Sad.

Excursions
Within the municipality, especially in **Sremski Karlovci** (an old city on the right bank of the Danube, 7½ miles/12km from Novi Sad), there are numerous important monuments and valuables: works of the 18th-century painters Jakov Orfelin and Teodor Kračun, the imposing 19th-century Patriach's Palace, the Grammar School buildings (1791), the Magistrates' Hall and the baroque 'Four Lions' fountain. One ornate, pale-gold building is topped by a sizeable stork's-nest. The Peace of Karlowitz, an Austro-Turkish treaty, was signed in the town in 1699.
In the **Fruška Gora** hills is the largest oasis of linden trees in Europe, and a variety of flora and fauna. Fruška Gora National Park contains a scattering of old Orthodox monasteries (see page 20).
On the outskirts of **Kovilj** village are a medieval monastery and well-known fishing marshes, such as Arkanj, abundant in all varieties of fish.

◆◆◆
SARAJEVO
Bosnia-Hercegovina
This city is inevitably associated with the violent event which led to World War I, when a young Bosnian nationalist shot dead Austria's Archduke Ferdinand in 1914.
Capital of Bosnia-Hercegovina, it straddles the narrow valley of the River Miljacka, surrounded by steep mountain slopes, and is about 120 miles (195km) southwest of Beograd or northwest of Titograd.
It was heavily bombed in World War II, but what remains is more than enough to make it worth a visit. In the words of an admirer from another Republic: 'When a visitor sees the small houses climbing up the slopes on both sides of the valley, with Oriental and middle-European buildings in the centre – just that first glimpse captures him or her for ever, and creates a wish to return.'
Sarajevo received its name in the 15th century from two Turkish words: Saraj Ovasi – 'field around the palace'. In the 16th century it acquired an architectural form which stayed almost unchanged until 1878, when Austria-Hungary occupied it and overlaid the Turkish intricacy with self-important,

CENTRAL YUGOSLAVIA

weighty buildings.
There are modern buildings in the western part, and peripheral industrial sites. Most of the interesting spots are in the old city centre, **Baščaršija** (Market Square) with the bustle of bazaars and cafés overlooked by the 135-foot (41m) minaret of the **Begova Džamija** (Gazi Husrev Beg Mosque) of 1531, from which the voice of the muezzin invokes Muslim prayers. The mosque has rich decoration, is adjacent to an Arabic clocktower (Sahat Kula), and opposite a *medresa* (theological school) with its 24 small domes and 12 high, needle-like chimneys. Sarajevo has 13 other important mosques. **Morića-Han,** once the biggest hotel of Turkish Sarajevo, is in a

Turkish-style costumes characterise a folk-dancing display in Sarajevo

big square in the same street and features an excellent restaurant with national cuisine. The street leads further to a small square with a Turkish fountain and to the **Kazandžiluk,** where centuries-old crafts are still plied by metalworkers and craftsmen in leather.
At Maršala Tita 106, the old **Serbian Orthodox church** has a superb iconostasis. Near by, at Maršala Tita 98, the **Jewish Museum** housed in an old synagogue reflects the history of the Sephardic Jews who arrived in Sarajevo, mostly from Spain, in the 16th century, as well as the tragic events of the 20th century.
In the fateful street near Princip's Bridge, at Svetozara Markovića 54, is the small **Mlada Bosna Muzej.** 'Young Bosnia' (Mlada Bosna) was the name of the nationalist organisation to

CENTRAL YUGOSLAVIA

which the assassin Gavrilo Princip belonged. The spot where Princip pulled the trigger is marked by a set of footprints.
Museum open: daily (except Sunday) 09.00-17.00 hrs in summer (until 14.00 hrs in winter).
The **Zemaljski Muzej Bosne i Hercegovine** (National Museum of Bosnia and Hercegovina) at Vojvode Putnika 7, contains local archaeological, ethnographic and natural history collections. Its main feature is a series of *'stećci'*, or Bogomil funerary monuments (see also page 22).
Open: Tuesday to Friday 09.00-17.00 hrs (weekends until 13.00 hrs).
Reached by trams 1, 2, 3 and 5 from the centre.

Accommodation
The newest hotel is the A category **Holiday Inn** (tel: (071) 215-688), with 714 beds. The **Hotel Evropa**, Vase Pelagica 5 (tel: (071) 532-722) is on the edge of Baščaršija and, though it needs renovation, it has the atmosphere of a good, old-world hotel. 396 beds, B category.

General Information: Turistički Informativni Centar, Jugoslovenske Narodne Armije (JNA) 50 (tel: (071) 25-151).

Winter Sports
Sarajevo hosted the 14th Winter Olympics in 1984, providing several new hotels and superbly-prepared skiing grounds on Jahorina, Igman, Bjelašnica and Trebević mountains. Somehow, the Olympics cachet failed to be sustained, the expected flood of foreign tourists hardly materialised, and there have been queries about maintenance.
A summary of facilities is given below:
Jahorina (6,276 feet/1,913m). At 20 miles (32km) from Sarajevo, it has excellent snow from mid-November to mid-April on what can be some of Yugoslavia's nicest slopes. There are several B category hotels, but the best are the **Bistrica** (tel: (020) 071-800), 284 beds, or the **Jahorina** (tel: (071) 800-124) – particularly its new part. 376 beds.
Trebević (5,345 feet/1,629m) is practically part of Sarajevo, and is easily reached by bus/car or by cable car from the centre. Although there is no skiing, the interesting Vučko sledge *piste* enables visitors safely to make the run where world champions compete.
Igman (4,928 feet/1,502m) is 15½ miles (25km) from Sarajevo. There are two ski-jumps of 230 feet (70m) and 295 feet (90m). Skiing is mainly cross-country. Accommodation is available in **Hotel Igman,** (tel: (071) 802-066). B category, 166 beds.
Bjelašnica (6,782 feet/2,067m), the highest and wildest mountain, is 19 miles (31km) from Sarajevo. It has two chair lifts, two baby-lifts, and several drag lifts. Maintenance has been described as 'worse than on Jahorina'. Accommodation can be had at **Medunarodni Omladinski Centar** (tel: (071) 802-044). 312 beds, B category, or at **Hotel Igman** (see above) with transport arrangements.

THE ADRIATIC COAST AND ISLANDS

Mountain and sea meet at Kotor

THE ADRIATIC COAST AND ISLANDS

Yugoslavia's long, indented coastline, with its offshore islands, is the country's principal attraction to visitors. Stretching from the Italian border in the north to the Albanian border in the south, it includes historic towns and cities, notably Dubrovnik and Split, popular beach resorts such as Poreč, the luxury complex of Sveti Stefan and magnificent scenery, as around Boka Kotorska (the Bay of Kotor).

What to See

◆
BIOGRAD
Croatia (map pages 44-5)
Biograd's Serbo-Croat name today means the same as when it was the ancient Roman Alba Civitas – 'White Town'. Though once a coronation city of Croatian kings and seat of bishops, it now has virtually no notable historic buildings, and the hints of past glories are seen only in excavation sites and the small museum with finds from offshore wrecks.
Nonetheless, it attracts visitors with its very clean sea and pebble beaches, fringed by pine and cypress forests, its marina, other yacht moorings, and its frequent ferries to Pašman Island, which overlooks the myriad Kornati isles, mystically seaward.
Near by is the brackish **Vransko Jezero** (Lake Vrana), a lure for anglers with its grey mullet, sole and eel.

Accommodation
Of several hotels, perhaps the best choice is the B category **Crvena Luka** (tel: (057) 83-108), which also has apartments. 500 beds in hotel, 302 beds in apartments.

THE ADRIATIC COAST AND ISLANDS

◆◆◆
BOKA KOTORSKA
(BAY OF KOTOR)
Montenegro (map above)
This 'Pearl of the Adriatic' gleams up to 20 miles (32km) inland, beyond three peninsulas, where an arm of the sea probes the seemingly impenetrable barrier of the mountains Orjen and Lovćen. The gulf branches into several smaller bays: Hercegnovi, Tivat, Morinj, Risan and Kotor. It is a unique ensemble of natural beauty, old and new towns, clean blue seawater, subtropical vegetation and mild sunny climate. But it has no sandy beaches on its narrow littoral.
Hercegnovi, beside the sharply curving fjord-like entrance to the bay, is the largest resort here. It mixes old and new – graciously gardened villas with incongruous modern apartment blocks. Best preserved historic monument is the fortress **Starigrad,** mainly Venetian on Turkish foundations. The town's other important fort was destroyed by the earthquake of 1979.

Hercegnovi also has a **museum and art gallery – 'Josip-Bepo Benković',** Mirka Komnenovića 9, (tel: (082) 43-967), with archaeological, ethnographic and modern art collections and a botanical garden of tropical and subtropical plants.
Open: daily 09.00-12.00 hrs and 17.00-20.00 hrs (summer); 09.00-12.00 hrs and 15.00-17.00 hrs (winter).
Between 1382 and 1918, the town was ruled in turn by Bosnians, Turks, Venetians, and

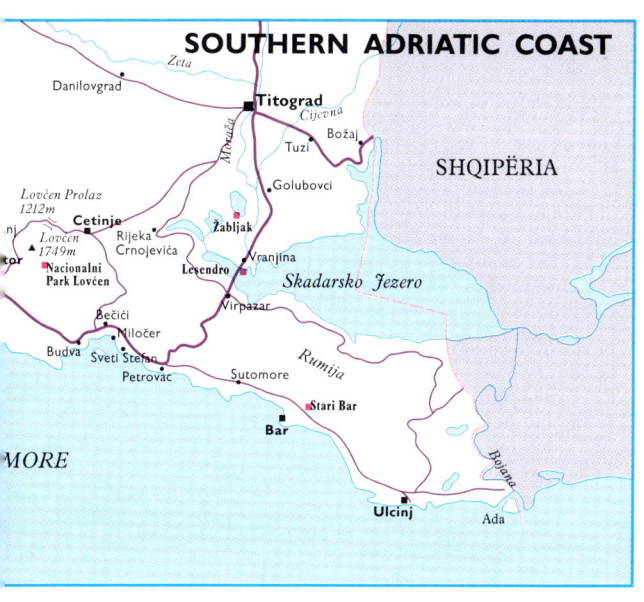

THE ADRIATIC COAST AND ISLANDS

SOUTHERN ADRIATIC COAST

even Napoleon. In the central part is the nice late-Gothic church of **St Michael.** A 15-minute walk away, by the **Hotel Plaža** (A category, 577 rooms, tel: (082) 52-151), is the 13th-century Orthodox **monastery of Savina.** Its exterior is interesting, with two churches, Byzantine and baroque, imposed over a small original chapel. Its treasury is worth seeing.

Settlements inwards along the bay shore from Hercegnovi include **Zelenika** (appropriately meaning green), **Bijela** (with its big shipyard) and **Kamenari** (car ferries across to Lepetane). From Turkish Cape is a spectacular view of the inner part of the Bay, and a narrow road curves round a cove to venerable **Risan,** associated with Illyrian mythology and with a ruined Roman palace that has well-preserved 2nd-century mosaics. Risan was destroyed by an earthquake around 1000, and the 1979 earthquake did considerable damage locally, but the **Hotel Teuta** (tel: (082) 72-318), 210 beds, swimming pool and private pebble beach, soldiers on.

Only about a mile (2km) further is **Perast,** mostly Venetian Gothic and baroque, but also badly damaged in the 1979 earthquake. This tiny place was, in the 17th and 18th centuries, a major naval education centre. Its graduates charted the Mediterranean coast, navigated the Venetian fleet at Lepanto, designed ports in the Baltic and, in the person of Admiral Matija Zmajević, commanded the

THE ADRIATIC COAST AND ISLANDS

Russian fleet of Peter the Great in a Baltic victory against the Swedes. A museum in a former palace attests.

Churches include the beautiful parish church of Sveti Nikola (15th – 17th centuries) and one dedicated to Our Lady of Rosarium (mainly a mausoleum).

A short boat-row from Perast are two lake islands. One hides the cypress-shaded Benedictine Abbey of Sveti Juraj (patron saint of all Boka Kotorska). The other is an artificial islet of stones, accommodating a graceful baroque church.

Kotor is tucked into a far corner of the bay under near-vertical slopes of Mount Lovćen. Most of the old town's buildings have been or are being restored after the 1979 earthquake. Its network of walls, originating in the 9th century on the slopes, amazingly survived this; the 12th-century cathedral has 17th-century restorations and an interesting treasury.

Narrow streets with Renaissance and baroque palaces lead to the port and an open-air food market on the city walls. The old town's **Naval Museum,** in the imposing Grgurina palace, has records going back to the 9th century. Along the shore is **Prčanj,** its big baroque church fronted by sculptures of important Montenegrins. There are beautiful gardens and a few 18th-century palaces and villas. After the ferry port of Lepetane is **Tivat,** which has an international airport. Major tourist town of the bay, it is like the new part of Hercegnovi,

with its palms and exotic flowers. For accommodation, the B category **Hotel Kamelija** (tel: (082) 61-300) is probably the best choice, with 95 rooms, private beach, sports grounds and swimming pool.

Two small islands near by are dedicated to tourism – **Sveti Marko,** home of a Club Méditerranée, and **Prevlaka** with its noted 'Flower Island' hotel settlement.

◆◆
BRAČ

Croatia (map pages 44-5)
The third largest of Yugoslavia's Adriatic islands, Brač is for those seeking the quiet life. The interior, with its pinewoods, vineyards and olive groves, is still mainly untouched by tourism – indeed, it is quite hard to get around unless you are a keen walker.

The island has been known since ancient times for its fine, creamy-white stone (it was used in Diocletian's Palace at Split), and some quarrying still goes on.

The main resorts are **Supetar,** on the north coast, and **Bol,** in the south. The latter has excellent sandy beaches, and a very good local museum in its Dominican monastery. **Postira** is a picturesque little town east of Supetar.

Accommodation

In Supetar there is the **Kaktus** (B category – tel: (058) 631-133), which has 224 beds. Bol is well supplied with hotels and apartments, many in the B range; there is also the A category **Elaphusa** (tel: (058) 635-288) with 358 beds.

THE ADRIATIC COAST AND ISLANDS

For those preferring to escape the crowds, there is the small B category **Hotel Vrilo** in Postira (tel: (058) 632-104), with only 42 beds.

◆◆
BUDVA
Montenegro (map pages 30-1)
A gem of a small walled town, Budva was once an island but is now linked to the Montenegrin mainland by a causeway. It was devastated by the 1979 earthquake, but is now back in the tourism business. In the colourfully-roofed town itself, with its elegant white campanile, there are short-stay apartments and rooms to let. But inclusive-tour, modern hotels and villas are near mainland beaches of coarse sand, small pebbles and rock, and may be among trees.

Budva was founded in the 4th century BC. Illyrian, Greek and Roman remains have been the subject of excavations. For the International Tourism Fair, theatre, musical and folklore events are staged around the resort. Watersports are available.

Accommodation
This includes the **Hotel Avala** (A category – tel: (086) 41-022), with 440 beds and somewhat resembling a car ferry's upper decks and bridge; the smaller and sympathetically designed **Hotel Mogren** (B category – tel: (086) 41-022); the attractive **Vile (Villas) Avala** (B category – tel: (086) 41-022), on a tree-spired hillside (98 beds); and the **Slovenska Plaža Holiday Village/Apartments,** (B category – tel: (086) 41-044) with 2,536 beds.

Nearby Resorts
Bečići. A modern resort with gardens and a spacious coarse sand/pebbly beach, it is three miles (5km) south of Budva, and practically an extension of its hotel 'suburb'.
Excursions from this area can include **Cetinje,** the former Montenegrin capital (see page 77), **Skadarsko Jezero** and a 'Pirate Cruise'.

As good as new: old Budva restored

THE ADRIATIC COAST AND ISLANDS

The tree-backed harbour at Cavtat, a pleasant spot for relaxation

◆◆
CAVTAT
Croatia (map pages 30-1)
Cavtat may remind some of small resorts on Italian or French rivieras which have not suffered much chrome-and-plate-glass commercialisation or crowding problems.

With various beaches on the peninsular rim of the Bay of Župa (Župski Zaliv), it is about 10½ miles (17km) southeast of Dubrovnik. Local vegetation is luxuriant, shading intimate villas and hotel amenities when the sun is strong. One disadvantage of Cavtat is the aircraft noise caused by Dubrovnik's Čilipi airport.

The mausoleum of the Račić family, created in the 1920s, is on a hill overlooking the town. It is the work of Yugoslavia's most celebrated sculptor, Ivan Meštrović, and is a coldly impressive monument.
Open: daily 10.00-12.00 and 15.00-18.00 hrs.

Also notable are the Bogišic scientific library, the baroque church of Sveti Nikola (containing Old Master paintings) and the Franciscan Monastery with its beautiful cloister.

Accommodation
Hotels include the **Croatia** (de luxe – tel: (050) 78-022), with 988 beds, above the town but with access down to a pebbly beach, not suitable for disabled; the traditional-style **Supetar,** (B category – tel: (050) 78-279), on the harbour front (58 beds); and several modern establishments on pebbly/rocky beaches outside town.

Excursions
These include a cruise along the Dubrovnik Riviera and a trip to the Konavlje wine-growing region, where colourful national costumes are still worn.

THE ADRIATIC COAST AND ISLANDS

Nearby Resorts
Plat, just northwest of Cavtat, is mainly a modern complex of hotels tucked in among hillside olive groves. (Note that the A-class **Hotel Ambassador,** tel: (050) 88-922, high above the pebbly and rock beach, is not suitable for the disabled. It has 570 beds.)

Srebreno is a small family resort among pines and tamarisk by a shingle beach. The **Vile (Villas) Srebreno,** B category, and described by one tour operator as 'modest', seem to have a more congenially local character than new eggbox structures elsewhere.

Mlini is a charming hamlet shielded to the north by high mountains and with a profusion of citrus trees, oleanders, olives and cypresses. Its pebbly beaches include a nudist one. The small 'modest' **Hotel Mlini** (B category – tel: (505) 486-053) achieves a nice pastiche of Mediterranean architecture, but is not suitable for the disabled.

◆◆
CRES-LOŠINJ
Croatia (map pages 50-1)
The Cres-Lošinj archipelago is a chain of around 30 small and larger islands in the north of the Adriatic with 310 miles (500km) of rugged coastline.
The bridge in Osor, on the isthmus between Cres and Lošinj, joins the two islands. The freshwater Vransko Jezero (Lake Vrana) on Cres, whose water surface is below sea-level, serves as a reservoir for all the islands throughout the year. There is a sumptuous variety of plants and pine forests, herbs and spices. Though the initial impression is of aridity, Cres is famous for its oak, beech and chestnut forests, and olive trees.
Lošinj is a kaleidoscope of colour all the year round. There are eucalyptus, acacia, agave, palms, orange and mandarin trees, and in May the island is covered with yellow broom, in June purple sage abounds.
The islands of the Cres-Lošinj archipelago lie secluded in Kvarner Bay. Alone, **Galiola** lies to the southwest, distinguished by its secluded lighthouse. The third largest island towards the south is **Unije**, then **Vele Srakane** and **Male Srakane**, and further south is **Susak**, famous for its vineyards. The 'Flower Island', **Ilovik**, is the next stop southwards. After Ilovik, a chain of beautiful islands offers excellent opportunities for day-excursions.

Sightseeing
On Cres island the little port of **Cres** has a well preserved heart, with town gate, defensive walls and towers, a number of churches (St Mary's having a fine Renaissance doorway), town hall and other historic buildings in various states of repair. **Osor** has a 15th-century bishop's palace and Renaissance cathedral.
The main resort of Lošinj is attractive Mali Lošinj with a Venetian tower (fine views), castle and historic churches. Worth seeing is **Creski Muzej** (the archaeological and cultural museum) in Cres, housed in the

THE ADRIATIC COAST AND ISLANDS

Palača Arsan and with many interesting items, including Roman amphorae and Venetian and Austrian sculpture.
Open: daily (except Monday) 09.00-11.00 and 15.00-17.00 hrs, April to October.
Other sights include the archaeological collection in Osor and the Valun Stone (an Old Croatian text inscribed on a stone with Latin translation) in the parish church in Valun village.

Accommodation

The hotels and camping sites are well situated near the towns, yet in the midst of an unspoiled environment. Hotels include:
Hotel Aurora, Suncana uvala, Mali Lošinj, (tel: (051) 861-324), 783 beds. B category.
Hotel Kimen, Cres, (tel: (061) 871-322). 420 beds. B category.
Hotel Punta, Veli Lošinj, (tel: (051) 861-022). 764 beds. B category.
For reservation information contact:
Tourist Association of the Comune, Cres-Lošinj, 51550 Mali Lošinj (tel: (051) 861-547).

Boating

The marinas in Mali Lošinj and Cres have all necessary equipment for yacht maintenance and repair.
Mooring space is available the whole year round, and boats of all sizes can be chartered there.

Entertainment

National festivities with folklore, choirs, and *klapa* (Dalmatian part songs) take place regularly. Disco clubs and outdoor dancing are popular.
Festivals in Mali Lošinj, Nerezine, Veli Lošinj, Cres and Susak are particular favourites.

For general information contact: **Turist Biro,** Cres (tel: (051) 871-133); **Turist Agency Privlaka,** Mali Lošinj (tel: (051) 861-426).

◆ CRIKVENICA AND SELCE

Croatia (map pages 50-1)
These twin resorts, sheltered by the island of Krk, are on the green and lush old 'Novi Vinodolski Riviera', famous for its health-giving air. There is a modern Thalassotherapy Institute.
Crikvenica has a mile-long (2km) beach of pebbles, shingle and rock, plus the option of man-made 'lido' facilities.
Nearby Selce has a touch of San Tropez about it, if imagination is used, with art galleries, craft shops and harbourside cafés.
Crikvenica's town centre is well geared up to the tourist trade, with a streetful of restaurants and much live music competing for your attention. One of the more interesting local developments is the conversion of a 15th-century convent into a B category hotel – the **Kaštel** (tel: (051) 782-044), 186 beds.
Other hotels include the imposing old-style category A **Therapia** (tel: (051) 781-046), providing accommodation for patients of the Thalassotherapy Institute (210 beds) the B category **Esplanade** (tel: (051)781-133), like a villa from vintage Somerset Maugham (161 beds); and the modern B category **Omorika** (tel: (051) 781-211), with 236 beds.

THE ADRIATIC COAST AND ISLANDS

◆◆◆
DUBROVNIK
Croatia (map pages 30-1)
World-famous now, Dubrovnik has held a proud place in the Mediterranean for centuries, and particularly as a medieval city-state with the motto: *'Libertas'* (Liberty).

The city was founded in the 7th century; as seen today it reflects its heyday in the 16th century, when it was an important commercial and cultural centre. Until 1918, Dubrovnik went by the name Ragusa (source of the word 'argosy'). It managed to retain its independence throughout centuries of foreign occupation elsewhere in the area, until it fell to Napoleon in 1806.

The monumental old city, mostly beautifully restored and preserved (though structural damage in the 1979 earthquake may mean that some buildings are under restoration), is for pedestrians only. A walk on and around its defensive walls (daily, 09.00-19.30 hrs – a small charge is made), in the challenge of strong sunlight, can be a good introductory exercise. Constructed between the 8th and 16th centuries, their perimeter is nearly 1¼ miles (2km), including steep flights of steps.

From the commanding heights of the walls, you look down on an ever-changing roofscape of red and yellow Romanesque tiles atop embellished creamy limestone, small Gothic-Renaissance palaces, secret courtyards, and the narrow stepped streets.

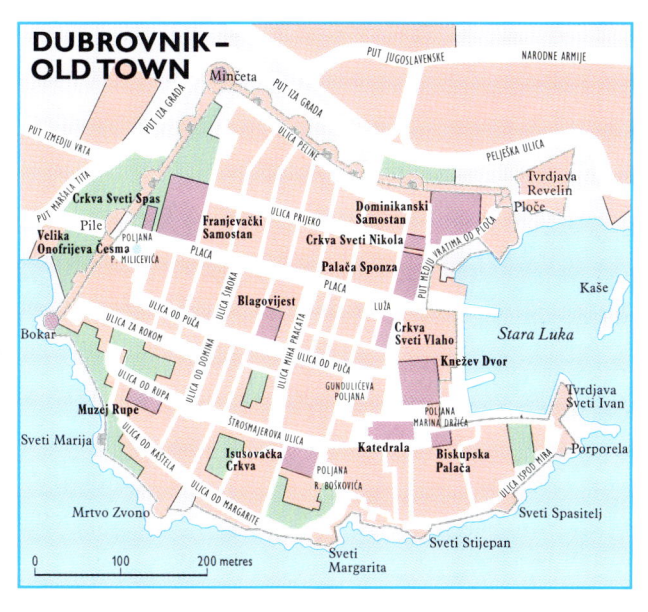

THE ADRIATIC COAST AND ISLANDS

The red roofs of Dubrovnik

Sightseeing in the Old Town
Knežev Dvor (Rector's Palace). This was the residence of the rector, who held office for just a month at a time as nominal head of the city-state. Built in the 15th century, it has furnished rooms to view and houses Dubrovački Muzej, (Dubrovnik Museum). *Open:* daily 09.00-13.00 hrs and 14.00-18.00 hrs April to October, and 09.30-13.00 hrs (not Sunday) the rest of the year.
Palača Sponza (Sponza Palace). The former customs house and mint, the 16th-century palace contains the city's archives.
Sveti Vlaha (St Blaise's Church). The baroque church (rebuilt after a fire) has the gilded statue of the patron saint of the city on the façade.
Franjevački Samostan (Franciscan Monastery). Situated just inside the entrance to the old city, the monastery is most notable for its cloisters and museum including artefacts from the old pharmacy founded in 1317.
Other sights include **Velika Onafrijeve Česme** (Onofrio's Fountain), the 15th-century **synagogue,** the baroque **cathedral**, the delightful **harbour,** and the wooded island and nature reserve of **Lokrum,** just off-shore.
For information on opening times, consult the tourist information centre (see page 39).

Accommodation
Sophisticated, well air-conditioned hotels – in lofty, cypress-spiked settings with good overviews of citadel and sea – include the A Category **Excelsior** (tel: (050) 23-566), with 393 beds, and **Argentina** (tel: (050) 32-524), 238 beds. The elegant Edwardian-style A category **Imperial** (tel: (050) 23-688), 254 beds, is nearer still, and with a public beach not far away from its gardens.
Tour operators' brochures feature the above and quite a selection of other accommodation in various categories. See also **Resort Area.**

Entertainment
The main evening activity is the *korso*, around dusk: promenading to see and be seen.
There are often concerts in historic settings in the old town, and international celebrities take part in the Dubrovnik Summer Festival, 10 July to 25 August; this can include Shakespeare plays in idealised settings, and its folklore fringe

THE ADRIATIC COAST AND ISLANDS

may feature characters striding about on stilts and declaiming in Old Croat, unintelligible even to locals.

Eating Out

Lunch, or dinner, could be at a shaded pavement table in the rather commercialised Prijeko Street. The **Ragusa Tavern,** taking Dubrovnik's Romanised name, is one of many private-enterprise Yugoslav establishments to do their own thing. The proprietor may buttonhole you with a spiel about the house special platter of freshest mussels, scampi, langoustine, sea bream and small sardines eaten like whitebait, with juicy mixed salad; you cannot beat the value, he says.

Resort Area

The modern, resort hotels are very properly outside the old city itself, though some pricy ones overlook it from walking distance. The Lapad peninsula is the main hotel area, much used by package tour companies.

The moderately priced **Dubravka** and **Babin Kuk** holiday villages are a 2½ mile (4km) bus-ride away, on a sea inlet by the Lapad peninsula. They comprise low-rise family hotels and a range of leisure and sports facilities among pines, olive groves and oleanders.

Shingly beaches, with comfortable bathing, have panoramic views of islands and coast mountains. In the middle of the Dubravka hotel village is an attractively designed shopping centre and promenade, with boutiques, a bank, entertainments, library, disco, snack bars, national restaurants, beer and wine cellar, medical care centre, and an open-air market.

Children can be kept happy all day by trained attendants at a play centre amid the trees. And there is a baby-sitting service for parents who dine out of their hotel – say, on the seaview terrace of the 19th-century **House of the Old Captain.**

Dubrovnik's international airport is well southeast of the town, along a road sometimes evocative of the Amalfi Drive on the Neapolitan Riviera of southern Italy.

Excursions

A wide choice of excursions includes many island centres **(Elafiti, Mljet, Korčula),** trips into the interior such as **Mostar** or **Medjugorje,** and other resorts up and down the coast such as nearby Cavtat.

General Information: Turistički Informativini Centar, Stradun, 50000 Dubrovnik, Placa 1 (tel: (050) 26-354).

A place to cool off in the Old Town

THE ADRIATIC COAST AND ISLANDS

◆
ELAFITI ISLANDS
Croatia (map pages 30-1)
The three main islands of this group of seven are Lopud, Šipan and Koločep. Their main charm is their natural beauty, with rich subtropical vegetation and cultivation of vines and olives making them green.
Šipan is the largest, though quietest of the three. There are traces of its Roman and medieval past in the town of Šipanska Luka and Sudjurad village. **Lopud** town on the island of the same name was the seat of the Dubrovnik republic in the 15th century and has an excellent local museum.
Koločep, the smallest of the inhabited Elafiti Islands, has remains of churches and a castle. Though the islands have a few hotels, they are mostly visited on a day trip.

◆◆◆
HVAR
Croatia (map pages 44-5)
Hvar is a charming little town and port on the island of the same name. Its herbal scents may greet you, in summer, even before you are close. It grows lavender and rosemary, grapes and olives.
Hvar has long been fashionable as a health resort. It attracts a high proportion of young people with its relaxed, informal atmosphere. Clients of inexpensive seafood restaurants can eat in the sea air on the stepped pavements outside them. There are bars and discos in town, and more sophisticated nightspots just up the coast. Beaches tend to be small and rocky; those on three islets just outside the port are reserved for naturists.
Badly damaged by Turks in 1571, earthquake-shaken in 1979, the town had to be restored completely (except for the fortress which withstood all Turkish attack). Hvar took shape around one of the largest – and most elegant – squares on the Adriatic.
The square ends in a small closed **harbour** (Mandrač) built in the 15th century for ships to shelter in. The 16th-century **cathedral** and the **bishop's palace** are at the west end. The **loggia** (part of the Palace Hotel) is in the square's northwest part and is one of the most beautiful public Renaissance buildings in Dalmatia.
The **theatre,** dating from 1612, was built in the former maritime arsenal.
The Franciscan **monastery** and its church, erected on a cape between two bays, have been completely preserved. The 15th-century church encloses a chapel which has interesting art exhibits.

Accommodation
Several good hotels include the A category **Palace** (tel: (058) 74-966), with 148 beds and its own pebbly/rocky beach. Not suitable for disabled visitors.

◆
IZOLA
Slovenia (map pages 50-1)
Once an island, as its name suggests, Izola is now a peninsula on the Bay of Koper (Koperski Zaliv). It harbours a fishing fleet, as it has for centuries.
There is sea angling for visitors,

THE ADRIATIC COAST AND ISLANDS

Hvar town, around its harbour

by courtesy of fishermen willing to help.
A vine-trellised bar/restaurant or two can be found near the quay, perhaps selling estimable *Refošk* wine. A few ornate buildings and remains of the Roman settlement, Haliaetum, provide other interest. The outer-town scene, particularly to the north, is partly industrial. In-town accommodations include pensions and rooms in private homes.

◆◆
KOPER
Slovenia (map pages 50-1)
Koper was Italian until a 1945 border-shift, and the town's old part is noticeably Venetian – though the (medieval) **governor's palace** in the theatrical main square, Titov Trg, has been dressed up with fancy turreting and emblazonment. The **cathedral**, from 1450, incorporates a mixture of styles; its belfry affords a view down on to a street pattern that could be in an antique print.

Works by Bellini and Carpaccio are among the fine Venetian art collection of the **Pokrajinski Muzej** (Civic Museum) in the baroque Palača Belgramoni-Tacco, Kidričeva 19.
Open: daily 09.00-13.00 and 17.00-19.00 hrs.
Inland, concrete-and-glass towers loom uncompromisingly over the suburban approach.

Excursions
Nearby **Ankaran** has parks with subtropical vegetation, a 500-year-old **Benedictine monastery** converted into a hotel, the cypress-flanked **Club Ankaran** tourist pavilions (B category), and beaches, some with coarse sand.
Hinterland hills are terraced with vineyards and tiny medieval towns. Excursions can be made to the frescoed church near **Hrastovlje**, to the vast stalactite cave systems of **Postojna** or **Škocjan**, Lipica's famous horse and stud farm, or the Slovenian capital **Ljubljana**.

THE ADRIATIC COAST AND ISLANDS

The medieval walled city of Korčula

♦♦♦
KORČULA
Croatia (map pages 44-5)
One of the greenest and most beautiful of the Adriatic islands, Korčula possesses a gem in the form of its town of the same name. This tiny walled city vies with some of the best for sheer beauty. Its street plan, which suggests the skeleton of a fish, gives the town protection from the north wind, and may go back to its original settlement by ancient Greek colonists.

There are many individual buildings worth looking at, not least the **cathedral,** dedicated to St Mark (Sveti Marko), built in the 13th to 16th centuries and reflecting the various architectural styles over those 300 years.

Many of its treasures and works of art are now housed in the 14th-century **Bishop's Palace.** *Open:* daily (except Sunday) 09.00-12.00 and 16.00-18.00 hrs June to September; 09.00-12.00 hrs October to May.

Look out also for the magnificent **Land Gate** of 1650, the Renaissance former **Prince's Palace,** the Gothic-Renaissance **Arneri Palace,** and the **Marco Polo House,** claimed to be the birthplace of the great Venetian explorer.

Four miles (6.5km) from Korčula town is **Lumbarda,** known for its golden *Grk* wine and its sculptors. It also has good beaches.

Accommodation
For sightseeing in Korčula town, the best bet is the **Korčula** (B category – tel: (050) 711-578), a small hotel (only 48 beds) on the quayside. Other hotels and apartments are a little out of town, above the beaches (often rocky or pebbly).

At Lumbarda, there are the

THE ADRIATIC COAST AND ISLANDS

Lumbarda hotel (B category – tel: (050) 712-622), with 290 beds, and the **Apartments Mala Glavica** (same management).

Entertainment
One of the sights of Korčula not to be missed is the famous *Moreška* (Moorish) dance, once performed only annually, but now a regular Thursday evening happening in summer in Korčula town. A less commercialised event is the *Kumpanjina*, a dance drama performed on 23 April in the island's largest town, Blato.

◆◆ KRK
Croatia (map pages 50-1)
Krk, in the Gulf of Kvarner, linked by road bridge to the mainland, is the largest of Yugoslavia's islands and, although there is some industry, a popular tourist spot.
The island has the usual complex history. It was settled by Illyrians and Greeks before becoming part of the Roman and Byzantine empires. It came under Venetian sway and was ruled for Venice by the powerful Croatian Francopan family for more than 300 years. There are many reminders of those days, such as the defensive walls of **Krk town,** the Frankopan Castle and the Bishop's Palace which now contains a collection of paintings. Other centres on the island are **Punat** (very crowded and touristy), and **Baška,** which has a good pebble beach. The latter is known for being where the oldest specimen of Glagolithic (Old Slavonic) script was discovered.

Accommodation
Krk town has several B category hotels, including the tiny **Marina** (tel: (051) 221-128) with 37 beds, the **Lovorka** (tel: (051) 221-022) with 180 beds and the **Koralj** (tel: (051) 221-044) with 400 beds. Baška has the B category **Corinthia** (tel: (051) 856-824) with 274 beds.

◆ LOVRAN
Croatia (map pages 50-1)
Charming little Lovran is a watering place once favoured by Austrian nobility.
Today, keen walkers might be attracted to the nearby wooded foothills of Mount Učka. Leisurely strollers will appreciate the attractive promenade which stretches 4½ miles (7km) from Lovran to Opatija.
The relaxed old town has some preserved walls and a parish church with interesting Gothic belfry and vault. The area around the tiny triangular harbour has much character. Nightlife is fairly demure. Restaurants have good reputations.

Accommodation
Hotel Excelsior (tel: (051) 712-233) is de luxe category with 370 beds. Standing in its seaside grounds on the north side of town, it was unobtrusively built in 1986 and has attracted friends and awards.
The **Belvedere** with 54 beds and **Beograd** with 191 beds (both tel: (051) 731-022) and the **Lovran** with 191 beds (tel: (051) 731-222) are all B category hotels, fairly centrally situated, and with traditional features.

THE ADRIATIC COAST AND ISLANDS

Makarska is a peaceful, attractive resort, suitable for families

◆◆ MAKARSKA

Croatia (map pages below)
Giving its name to a riviera, Makarska is a delightfully atmospheric port displaying narrow stone streets, congenial restaurants, a wide and palmy promenade with terraces, and a Franciscan monastery, whose museum, at Zrtava Fasizma 1, houses a major **collection of seashells** from all parts of the world.
Open: daily, 09.00-12.00 and 17.00-20.00 hrs July to October; 11.00-12.00 hrs February to June and November. Closed December and January.

THE ADRIATIC COAST AND ISLANDS

The gently curving harbour and resort area are protected from north winds by the giant Biokovo mountain, and from seaborne disturbance by the islands of Hvar and Brač. The town has an open-air stage, and claims to be a centre for almost every sport.

Accommodation

Fortunately, the rather starkly modern holiday hotels are built outside the town, near beaches, but the characterful B category **Hotel Biokovo** (tel: (058) 612-244) with 113 beds, is by a small pedestrian area in the town centre.

Nearby Resorts

Tučepi (southeast) and Baška Voda and Donja Brela (northwest) are beautifully situated in pinewoods by pebbly or shingly beaches. **Donja Brela** has a small fishing port and a coastal promenade leading to **Baška Voda** with its freshwater springs. **Tučepi**, with some rebuilt baroque houses, was one of Yugoslavia's first coastal places chosen for post-war holiday hotels.

A little further southeast, one of the pleasantest resorts on the Makarska Riviera is **Podgora**, shielded by the Biokovo (White Mountain) massif to the rear and

THE ADRIATIC COAST AND ISLANDS

looking seaward towards the islands of Brač and Hvar, visitable on boat excursions. The World War II Yugoslav (Partisan) navy was founded here in 1942 (there is a modern monument). With oranges and lemons in its gardens, Podgora is a now peaceful and relaxing place for families with young children. Pretty **Igrane,** a few miles to the south, spills down a hill to the sea; and inland there are Biokovo mountain villages for sturdy walkers.

Accommodation in Podgora: **Minerva** (tel: (058) 625-333) is A category and has 330 beds. The **Aurora** (tel: (058) 625-111), 280 beds, **Mediteran** (tel: (058) 625-155), 346 beds, and **Podgorka** (tel: (058) 625-266), 414 beds, are all B category. The latter, traditionally styled and on a beach near the village and harbour, does not have steps, and is therefore suitable for disabled visitors.

◆
MLJET
Croatia (map pages 44-5)
This island is a destination for nature-lovers. Its dense pine forests are thought to pre-date man and, with the two salt lakes (Malo Jezero and Veliko Jezero) form the Nacionalni Park Mljet (Mljet National Park – see **Peace and Quiet** page 92). On an island in Veliko Jezero is a one-time Benedictine monastery which is now a recently renovated hotel, the **Melita** (tel: (050) 329-71). Mljet has traces of habitation since prehistoric times, the most impressive remains being those of the 5th-century Roman palace in Polače.

◆
NOVIGRAD
Croatia (map pages 50-1)
Novigrad is a delightful-looking little Istrian promonotory and port which, despite its name (meaning 'new town'), dates back to before Christ.
It has Gothic, Renaissance and baroque buildings, the restored basilica of Sveti Pelagija from the 13th century, and a collection of ancient Croatian artefacts.

Eating Out
Restaurants around the relaxed atmospheric waterfront range from the cosy-characterful to the riviera-stylish. The unsmiling 'welcome' from some staff members can be disconcerting in a location so near Italy. Delightful inland hill villages and towns towards Motovun (see page 65) produce good Cabernet red and homely white wines, around what is habitat for seasonal mushrooms and truffles (with aphrodisiac reputation). Eating thereabouts is thought congenial.

Accommodation
For local atmosphere, the 'modest' **Hotel Emonia** (B category, tel: (532) 51-14) has a nice position by the marina, and 76 beds, and there are pretty village apartments in quiet streets away from the centre. Near pebbly and rocky beaches, just outside the village, are two low-rise, modern 'B' hotels, the unexceptional **Laguna** (tel: (053) 59-026) with 438 beds, and the well-equipped **Maestral** (tel: (053) 31-472), 748 beds and with about the exterior charm of an airport terminal.

THE ADRIATIC COAST AND ISLANDS

The promenade in stately Opatija

◆ OMIŠ

Croatia (map pages 44-5)
A small town and harbour at the mouth of the river Cetina, 15½ miles (25km) south of Split, Omiš has some resort facilities by several beaches. It was a Croatian feudal fortress conquered by 14th-century Venetians, and a pirate stronghold.
Some of its gates and a tower have been preserved, as has an impressive fort on a hill above town. On the west bank of the Cetina is the pre-Romanesque church of Sveti Petar (St Peter), dating from the 10th century. The 17th-century parish church is an important baroque monument, and a nearby Renaissance building houses the town's archaeological and ethnographic collections.
Accommodation in private homes can be negotiated, as elsewhere. **Radmanone Mlin** (mill) and **Šarin Otok island** are excursion spots in the Cetina river canyon.

◆◆ OPATIJA

Croatia (map pages 50-1)
Opatija achieved royal acclaim as a health and pleasure resort when it took the fancy of Austria's Emperor Franz Josef and his court in the mid-1800s. It developed auspiciously, and the *fin-de-siècle* grandeur of some hotels and other buildings is still to be seen in various colonnaded balconies, terracings, and ornament. Unfortunately, progress in post-World War II days – before Yugoslavia embraced its current greater enthusiasm for environmental care – implanted a few incongruous modern hotel blocks.
Nevertheless, at least seven hotels have swimming pools with heated seawater (there being also a noted Institute of Thalassotherapy), among facilities which make a winter stay enjoyable. And there is a

THE ADRIATIC COAST AND ISLANDS

spirited contemporary scene in night-clubs, bars, restaurants and the casino.

Colourful gardens complement the picture at this major resort, which is sheltered by the wooded 5,000-foot (1,400m) Mount Učka. The 'beach' is a wide concrete quay-cum-promenade, five miles (8km) long.

Opatija is a well-known congress centre. It stages an annual regatta, several tennis tournaments, and the Summer Festival of Music, which appeals to catholic tastes.

It is a good starting-point for trips to **Pula** (Roman monuments), numerous other attractions around the Istrian peninsula, **Venice,** the **Lipica** Horse Stud, the caves of **Postojna** and **Škocjan,** and various islands.

Accommodation

The following B category hotels have traditional character: **Hotel Kvarner** with **Villa Amala** annexe (tel: (051) 711-211), 162 beds; **Imperial-Atlantic** (tel: (051) 712-533), 289 beds; **Slavija** (tel: (051) 711-811), 221 beds; **Palme** (tel: (051) 711-823), 187 beds; **Kristal** (tel: (051) 711-333), 233 beds; and **Dubrovnik** (tel: (051) 712-444), 173 beds.

Modern hotels (which often appear in tour operators' brochures) include the cuboid de luxe **Ambasador** (tel: (051) 712-211) with 541 beds; the A category **Admiral** (tel: (051) 711-533) with 344 beds; and the *éminence-grise* **Hotel Paris** (B category – tel: (051) 711-911), 168 beds.

◆◆
OREBIĆ

Croatia (map pages 44-5)

Orebić is the main resort on the Pelješac peninsula. This giant-lizard's tongue of land protrudes more than 37 miles (60km) from the mainland north of Dubrovnik, and produces hearty wines (notably *Dingač* and *Postup*), oysters, and seafarers, who eventually retire there, as they have for centuries.

The siren lure of Orebić, on Pelješac's south coast, now attracts sun-seeking visitors in the wake of sea captains. Along the shore its houses line up in good order, with a church spire amidships, like a mainmast. Some of them are unofficial museums, displaying treasured flotsam and jetsam from world voyages.

By a cypress-guarded old sailors' cemetery above the town, the **Franjevački Samostan** (Franciscan monastery) contains a wealth of venerable shipping tackle, bric-à-brac and maritime paintings. The patient monk-in-charge may show visitors its special pride, a fine violin of indefinite provenance, while another duty-monk serves the monastery's port-type wine. *Open:* daily 10.00-12.00 and 16.00-18.00 hrs.

Accommodation

The following B category hotels are near pebbly or rocky beaches: **Bellevue** (tel: (050) 713-188), 139 beds; **Orsan** (tel: (050) 713-026), 196 beds; **Rathaneum** (tel: (050) 713-022), 392 beds.

THE ADRIATIC COAST AND ISLANDS

Excursions
There are oyster and mussel beds near the twin small communities of **Mali Ston** and **Veliki Ston,** on the narrowest (eastern) part of the peninsula. Among Ston's many monuments are an impressive network of defence walls, the Gothic former office of the (Dubrovnik) Republic, the Bishop's Palace, and a Franciscan cloister. Frequent ferry services from Orebić operate to **Korčula,** and (in high season) there are boat transfers to a naturist island.

◆◆
PIRAN
Slovenia (map pages 50-1)
In this ancient peninsular town, *'Lassa Pur Dir'* (Let Them Talk) is the motto inscribed on the wall of what is now the Tourist Office – said to have been placed there provocatively by an Italian merchant, in response to local gossip, when he built the house for his mistress in ornamental Tartinijev Trg (Tartini Square).

Piran harbour: a touch of Venice

A bronze statue of Tartini, the famous violinist and composer, born in Piran in 1692, plays silent music in the square. His violins and manuscripts are in the **Obalni Galerij Piran** (Coastal Gallery), which also has departments representing local seamanship, fishing, and the history of the Piran salt works. *Open:* daily 10.00-12.00 and 18.00-20.00 hrs.

The **cathedral** on a hill, which has a fine view of the Bay of Trieste (Tržaški Zaliv), gained its present baroque appearance when the 17th-century bell tower was completed, in imitation of St Mark's campanile in Venice. Behind the Renaissance façade is a rich interior with altars and canvases from the Venetian school and 18th-century sculptures.

Accommodation
Hotels include the B category **Piran** (tel: (066) 73-651), 116 beds; and the C category **Sidro** (tel: (066) 75-292), 97 beds in Tartinijev Trg.

◆◆◆
POREČ
Croatia (map pages 50-1)
Poreč is the biggest tourist resort in attractive wine-growing Istria, if not all Yugoslavia. Its main resort hotels are ranged unobtrusively along the coast on either side of the historic Istrian peninsular town.

The holiday complexes are mini-resorts in themselves: **Lanterna** is a new resort on a wooded peninsula, six miles (10km) from Poreč, with terraced stone beaches and a naturist beach; **Červar-Porat** is

49

THE ADRIATIC COAST AND ISLANDS

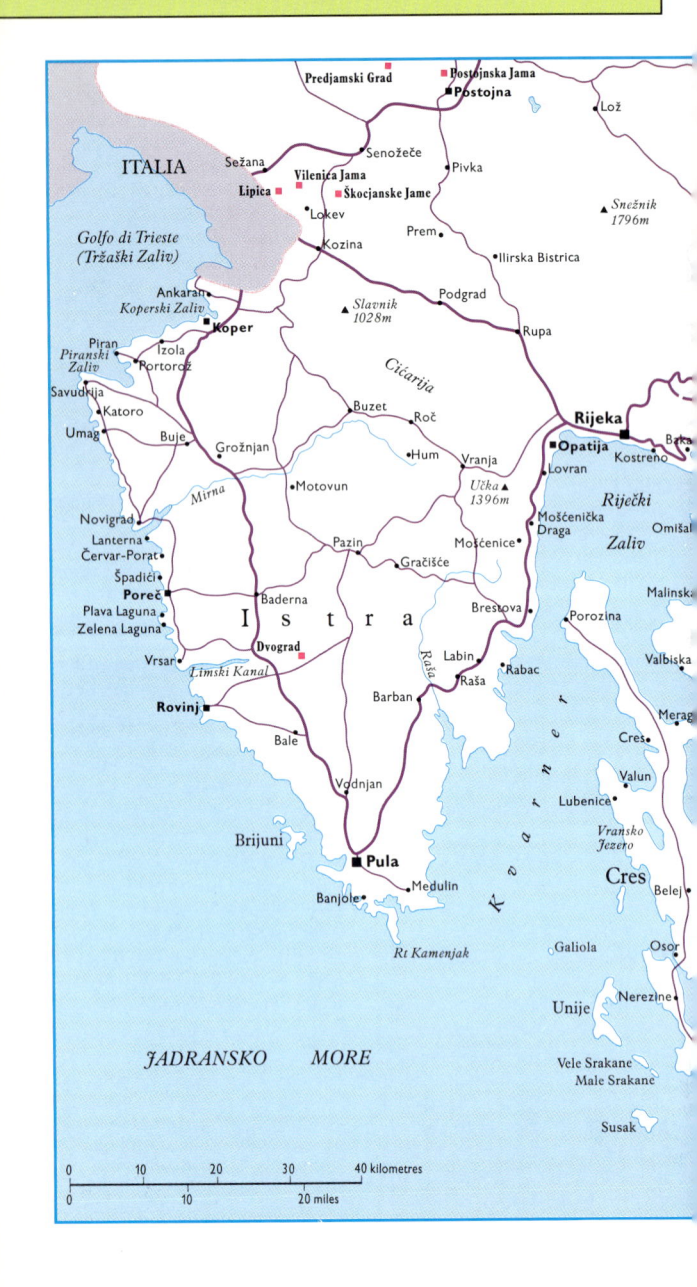

THE ADRIATIC COAST AND ISLANDS

ISTRIA AND THE KVARNER

THE ADRIATIC COAST AND ISLANDS

for sailing folk; **Materada-Špadići** has family villas and a mainly rocky beach; **Pical** is a modern hotel complex. **Zelena Laguna** (the 'Green Lagoon'), by a pebbly and rocky beach and shaded by pines, is a lively sports and entertainments centre with some commercial aspects of hamburger-culture. Escapists may prefer amenities on the wooded island of **Sveti Nikola**, where there are hotels looking across to old Poreč over the water.

Traditional Poreč (which goes back to Roman times) has narrow streets, pleasant patterns of shuttered Venetian houses with the occasional gaudy splash of a souvenir shop, and a leisurely harbour-front. The 6th-century **Basilica of Euphrasius**, down a side-turn off Ljubljanska, is a quite remarkable monument, featuring spectacular interior gold mosaic frescos and a museum.

Accommodation

Mass tourism has taken over here, with the hotels catering for package tour visitors. The independent traveller would be well advised to seek accommodation elsewhere on the coast. On the island of Sveti Nikola, however, there is the B category **Fortuna** hotel (tel: (053) 31-427).

Excursions

There is reasonable access to **Motovun** (see page 65), **Limska Kanal** (se page 66), Lipica horse stud farm, **Postojna** stalactite caves, **Ljubljana** and even (by hydrofoil, boat or coach) **Venice**.

◆
PORTOROŽ
Slovenia (map pages 50-1)

'Port of Roses', Portorož lives up to its name with flower-filled terraced parks and gardens side by side with yacht marina and boatyard. With its big-money casino, this is one of the coast's most sophisticated (and expensive) centres.

Across an inlet from a semi-commercial area is Seča Point Park's extensive Forma Viva exhibition, in which native and foreign sculptors, participating in an annual sculptors' symposium, have carved out scores of figures and motifs in white marble.

Accommodation

The imposing **Grand Hotel Palace** (A category – tel: (066) 73-541), 396 beds, with its thermal baths, is mainly for independent clients.

Tour operators feature in-town hotels **Slovenija**, (A category), and **Riviera** (B category), together having 805 beds (tel: (066) 73-051), and man-made and imported sand beach. The **Bernardin** (tel: (066) 75-271), 465 beds, with nearby **Villas Park** (tel: (066) 75-271), 478 beds (both B category), are built close to a small harbour and the 15th-century bell tower of St Bernardin Monastery.

Not far away, the modern white **Grand Hotel Emona** (A category – tel: (066) 75-271), 420 beds, descends a dozen floors to (man-made) beach level at a similar sloping angle to adjacent limestone cliffs – a brave effort at large-scale design, with a coolly spacious interior.

THE ADRIATIC COAST AND ISLANDS

The Roman amphitheatre in Pula

◆
PRIMOŠTEN

Croatia (map pages 44-5)
Primošten is a pretty fishing village, now expanded to a substantial resort, on an island connected to the mainland. It is considerably bigger than chic Sveti Stefan down in Montenegro (see page 61), and with richer fishing waters – thus it has not needed to follow the southern village's example of turning itself into a resort, lock, stock and barrel.
Picture-book houses cluster below its restored 15th-century church. Resort hotels are on separate mainland sites, amid thick evergreen woods and by pebble and rock beaches whose edges may be a metre or two above sea of some depth.

Accommodation

Among tour operators' hotels are **Zora-Slava** (A category – tel: (059) 70-022) with 700 beds, and **Raduča** (B category – tel: (059) 70-022), with 186 beds.

Excursions

By boat you can visit **Zlarin Island** and **Krapanj,** where coral workers and sponge divers operate, or have a Fish Picnic, or go to **Hvar** island; by road, destinations can be **Krka Slap** (Krka Waterfalls), or **Trogir** and **Split.**

◆◆
PULA

Croatia (map pages 50-1)
Pula has its magnificent amphitheatre and temple remains from Roman times, and pleasant tourist settlements on its coastal outskirts. However, as the largest town in Istria, it is also an industrial centre – and has not *in itself* the beach resort ambience which may be inferred from the highly selective descriptions of it in some commercial brochures. By various inlets towards the southern extremity of Istria's west coast, it must have been an

THE ADRIATIC COAST AND ISLANDS

irresistible prize for the Romans who built triumphal monuments in the 1st century AD. Centuries earlier, so says the legend of the Argonauts, refugees from Colchis, home of Medea, settled here.

But the 20th century brought a heavier-duty shipyard, stark concrete edifices, and traffic fumes – though these do not diminish the dramatic presence of the 1st-century **amphitheatre's** great arched circular wall of tawny stone, and what remains of its original seating for 23,000. Built for circuses and contests involving gladiators and wild animals, it is now a venue for bloodless folklore shows, concerts, and the Yugoslav Film Festival (last week in July).
Open: daily 08.00-20.00 hrs.
Down the street is the **Arheološki Muzej Istre** (Archaeological Museum), Mate

A shady refuge in Rab old city

Balote 3, with Roman works of art and craft and objects from very early periods and from all over Istria.
Open: daily 09.00-19.00 hrs.
The 1st century BC **Porta Aurea** (triumphal arch) in Ulica Prvomajska is one of several massive structures incorporated into the fabric of Pula. It was built in tribute to the Sergi family, who continued to be prominent for at least 13 centuries. The **Temple of Augustus** is in Trg Republike, the square on the site of the Roman forum. Inside are the best of Pula's Roman finds.

Accommodation

In town is the augustly balconied Victorian-style **Hotel Riviera** (B category – tel: (052) 41-166, 110 beds). Near pebble, shingle, rocky or man-made beaches along the coast are hotels offered by tour operators, including the **Park** (B category –

THE ADRIATIC COAST AND ISLANDS

tel: (052) 24-611, 242 beds); **Brioni** (A category – tel: (052) 34-888, 444 beds); **Splendid** (B category – tel: (052) 23-390, 324 beds); and **Zlatne Stijene** (tel: (052) 34-811), 700 beds).
Medulin, around the turn of Istria's southeastern point, is a self-contained complex with hotels, villas and camping.

Excursion
The peaceful **Brijuni (Brioni) Islands,** which have been designated a National Park, can quickly be visited from a local port. The biggest, Veliki Brijun, was a perennial favourite of Marshal Tito, and here he entertained a veritable Who's Who of famous visitors. Visitors' movements are restricted however, because of the fragility of the islands' ecosystem.

♦♦♦
RAB
Croatia (map pages 50-1)
Rab belongs to the group of Kvarner islands in the northern Adriatic. Its charming main town has a skyline of four slender campanili along the old town walls and, with its twisting, narrow Mediterranean streets, preserves many fine buildings. They include the splendid Romanesque-Gothic cathedral (Sveta Marija), other medieval churches (13th-century), the **Loggia** (a former law court), and palaces with beautiful doorways. **Sveti Justina** church includes a museum with a religious art collection.
A particular attraction is **Komrčar Park** which has a monument to Belia, the head-forester who laid it out. Pinewoods descend to the sea and beaches.

Accommodation
Hotel Padova (B category – tel: (051) 771-444), 354 beds, has a main building and villas.
Hotel International (B category – tel: (051) 771-266), with 247 beds is on the harbour front of the old town.
Other hotels include the B category **Imperial** (tel: (051) 771-522), 260 beds, and **Istra** (tel: (051) 771-134), 192 beds; and the D category **Beograd** (tel: (051) 771-340) with 91 beds.

Entertainment
There is plenty to see and do locally, including folklore and theatrical performances, films and various sports. Yachting visitors should report to the harbourmaster's office.

Excursions
Boats sail to the 'Island of Love', **Suka Punta,** and to the naturist beach – one of the first on the Adriatic coast. There are also trips to many island and mainland centres, including **Lun,** an idyllic fishing village on the island of **Pag,** renowned for smoked ham, cheese, wine and honey.

♦
RABAC
Croatia (map pages 50-1)
An important resort, largely purpose-built since World War II, Rabac is sheltered by wooded hills and headlands, looks out from pebble or rock beaches towards the island of Cres across clear blue-green sea, and has some local character around its fishing port. But tour operators' ecstatic

THE ADRIATIC COAST AND ISLANDS

The fishing village of Rabac has developed into a modern resort

descriptions may reflect enthusiasm as to the amount of business afforded by its extensive hotel capacity. Diversions include watersports, tennis and crazy golf; there is plenty of music and dancing at night.

Accommodation
Several hotels, mainly B category, feature in tour operators' brochures; Yugotours in particular has the highly organised **Club Hotel Castor** (B category – tel: (052) 872-322), 450 beds, with children's programme run by a British 'Auntie', a resident band six nights a week, talent shows, etc. For those seeking smaller hotels, there are the C category **Istra** (tel: (052) 872-243) with 75 beds and D category **Primorka** (tel: (052) 872-217) with 52 beds.

Excursions
Northwards up the coast the Opatija Riviera begins, with the lived-in atmosphere, fishermen's nets, and seaweed tang of **Mošćenička Draga**, and the fetching walled townlet of **Mošćenice** on a green hillside above it.

Much of the western Istrian peninsula coast is within easy driving distance across attractive countryside, featuring beautiful hill villages. Inland excursions north can include **Ljubljana, Postojna Caves,** and the **Lipica** horse centre.

◆
RIJEKA
Croatia (map pages 50-1)
Yugoslavia's biggest port, and a very developed industrial centre with shipyards and refineries, Rijeka has historic monumental appeal in its old town. The 18th-century domed church of **Sveti Vid** (St Vitus), for instance, was obviously modelled after Santa Maria della Salute in Venice.

The **town hall** is from the 15th century (with later reconstructions), as is the **town clock** across the square. Two Austrian emperors are commemorated by busts in the 18th-century clocktower.

The **Pomorski i Istorijski Muzej Hrvatskog Primorja** (Maritime Museum and Historical Museum of the Croatian Seaside), Zrtava Fasizma 18, houses costumes, weaponry and furniture in stuccoed rooms.

Open: Tuesday to Saturday 09.00-13.00 hrs.

The hilltop **fortress of Trsat** is a largely 13th-century foundation,

THE ADRIATIC COAST AND ISLANDS

rebuilt in the 19th century. From here there is a fine view over the whole Kvarner Bay. The site is used for a restaurant and open-air theatre.

Accommodation
Rijeka has a rather indifferent selection of in-town accommodation considering its size, the best choices being the hotels **Bonavia** (A category – tel: (051) 33-744) with 289 beds, or **Jadran** (B category – tel: (051) 421-600) with 143 beds.

Excursions
Characterful and smaller resorts of the Kvarner Riviera are close at hand.
Rijeka is a transit point for inland excursions as well as trips to the islands of **Cres** and **Lošinj**, **Rab**, and (via the modern 'Tito's Bridge') **Krk.**

General Information: Turistički Informativni Biro, 51000 Rijeka, Trg Republike 9 (tel: (051) 33-909).

♦♦
ROVINJ
Croatia (map pages 50-1)
Beautiful as it is, Rovinj does not seem to require as much reverence as, say, Dubrovnik. It lets its hair down, and its washing hang out across narrow streets, with no inhibition, and its waterfront has a jaunty independent air.

A **Venetian bell tower** rises in austere white elegance above the colourful jumble of the town. There is no escaping the sight of this 197-foot (60m) campanile of St Euphemia's Cathedral (Sveta Eufemija) from almost every angle and contour of the densely-roofed peninsular mound it surmounts. Traditionally, it was an important navigation aid to sailing-ships at sea. Its weather-vane is a large gilt figure of St Euphemia. Seafarers could espy whether the saint was facing towards them in safe welcome – or whether the wind had turned her back on them, indicating danger.
A Franciscan monastery, Renaissance and baroque palaces, a painting gallery and the Institute of Marine Biology are among bigger set pieces in a scene interspersed with some gaudy souvenir shops, unpretentious boutiques, tavernas, cafés, bars, and stalls of the gypsy market. The Summer Festival has a theatrical setting. Offshore islands including **Crveni Otok** (Red Island) and **Katarina** are visitable by boat.

Accommodation
This is modern and, fortunately, away from the old town, among pine trees.
By a rocky beach and yacht marina, the **Hotel Park** (A category – tel: (052) 811-077, 464 beds), enjoys a particularly fine view of the medieval cluster shimmering across the water.
The **Hotel Istra** (A category – tel: (052) 813-055, 700 beds), on a rocky/pebbly beach of Crveni Otok island, has a somewhat nautical air.
The **Villas Rubin** (B category – tel: (052) 811-055, 3,242 beds), provide pleasant family accommodation and amenities by a beach just over 1¾ miles (3km) from Rovinj.

THE ADRIATIC COAST AND ISLANDS

♦♦ ŠIBENIK
Croatia (map pages 44-5)
Long a leading Dalmatian centre of trade and culture, Šibenik is a fishing port and naval base on the Krka river estuary.

The great glory of the fortified old town is the **Cathedral** of St James (Sveti Jakov), which took over 100 years to build. The 74 life-sized heads on the outside of its three apses include some reminiscent of ancient Greek busts, though others apparently represent sea captains, merchants, and other local characters from everyday 15th-century life.

Begun in 1431, the church contains exceptional Gothic and Venetian-style work by the local master Juraj Dalmatinac (George the Dalmatian) and by Nicholas of Florence.

In the same square, Trg Republike, is an arcaded loggia in pure Renaissance style. Its central column once served as a pillory to which offenders were tied in public disgrace. Next door is the **Rector's Palace** which now serves as the **Town Museum** with a collection of local finds from Neolithic to early medieval times.
Open: Tuesday to Friday 12.00-13.00 hrs and 19.00-21.00 hrs, and Saturday and Sunday 10.00-12.00 hrs.

Accommodation
In town is the **Hotel Marjan** (B category – tel: (059) 22-480). Outlying, on pebbly/man-made beaches, is the **Solaris Hotel** settlement used by tour operators (tel: (059) 338-44).

Excursions
Nearby destinations include **Krka Slap** (the Krka Waterfalls) and the Krka river canyon, and **Manastir Visovac** (Visovac Monastery) on a lake island.

General Information: Nacionalni Park Krka, 59000 Šibenik, Ive Lole Ribara 31 (tel: (059) 27-720).

♦ SLANO
Croatia (map pages 30-1)
In a sea inlet looking out at wooded peninsulas, Slano means 'salty'. It has a pebble beach safe for children, plus deep water swimming from rocks.

Of sightseeing interest are the 5th-century sarcophagi, 14th-century Franciscan Monastery, Rector's Palace, 15th-century Church of St Jeronimo and 18th-century Ohmučević Palace.

A traditional fair is held annually on 2 August, when the *lindo*, a folk dance, is performed in full costume.

Orašac is a peaceful village not far away – slightly inland, and at the foot of wooded mountain slopes. Close to the village is a ruined castle, and above it a small Dominican monastery from 1690. About half a mile (1km) away, through the pines, is the seafront **Soderini Holiday Village**.

Accommodation
Hotel Admiral (B category – tel: (050) 87-202) is a nicely designed hotel on the waterfront with 599 beds.
Hotel Osmine (B category – tel: (505) 87-244) is smaller (310 beds).

THE ADRIATIC COAST AND ISLANDS

Excursions
Nearby **Trsteno** has a remarkable park with exotic subtropical plants, various tree and shrub specimens in an arboretum, and, at the park's entrance, two enormous plane trees from the 16th century. Other destinations are the fishing village of **Veliki** and **Mali** (Big and Little) **Zaton; Vjetrenica Jama** (Vetrenica Cave) in the Popovo Polje region; and oriental **Mostar**.

♦♦♦
SPLIT
Croatia (map pages 44-5)
For a 'collector' of cities, Split is a fascinating, large, multi-faceted gem, even if occasionally flawed. Among its archaeological highlights are the well-preserved relics of the Roman Emperor Diocletian's vast palace from about AD300, its underground halls now used as galleries and souvenir shops. It was Diocletian – himself Dalmatian-born – who put Split on the map, when he chose the site for his retirement. After the departure of the Romans, refugees from Slav invasion made their homes in the palace and the town grew from there. Business and industry is much pursued around this major port and economic centre of Dalmatia, as evinced by factories in its outskirts. Split has one of the world's most productive shipyards.
Its friendly, lively people are local assets. Though some create noise disproportionate to the power of their auto-cycles, unofficial young troubadours from the university provide pleasanter sounds as they strum guitars on café terraces by Roman temple columns.

Sightseeing
Diocletian's Palace. The substantial remains of the palace include the walls and towers; three large gates (Zlatna, Vrata, Srebrna Vrata and Željezna Vrata – Golden, Silver and Iron Gates); the peristyle; Temple of Jupiter, (now the cathedral baptistry); and the main square fronting Diocletian's Mausoleum (now the cathedral). Robert Adam, the 18th-century British architect, used features of them as examples for the 'new' classical style.
Medieval city. In Narodni Trg (National Square), just outside the palace precincts, is the triple-walled loggia belonging to the 15th-century town hall,

Market within Diocletian's Palace

THE ADRIATIC COAST AND ISLANDS

which today houses the **Etnografski Muzej** (Ethnographic Museum). On the east side of the square is the town guard loggia, and above it a tower with Renaissance clock and a small Gothic belfry. Above the Golden Gate is a small but interesting early Croatian church, from the 9th century.

Museums
Arheološki Muzej
(Archaeological Museum), Zrinjsko-Frankopanska 25, has a collection of locally excavated Illyrian, Greek, Roman and medieval objects.
Open: daily (except Monday) 09.00-13.00 and 17.00-20.00 hrs winter; 09.00-13.00 hrs (Sunday 10.00-12.00 hrs) summer.
Etnografski Muzej, Iza Lože 1. Local crafts and costumes.
Open: daily 09.00-13.00 and 18.00-20.00 hrs June to October, 09.00-13.00 hrs the rest of the year.
Galerija Meštrović (Meštrović Gallery), Šetalište Moše Pijade 46. Dedicated to the work of Yugoslavia's best known sculptor.
Open: daily 10.00-15.00 hrs summer; 10.00-17.00 hrs winter.
Muzej Grada Splita (Museum of Split), Papalićeva. More notable for the building than the contents – city relics. The local 15th-century master Juraj Dalmatinac built the ornate Gothic-style palace of the Papalić family. Altered in Renaissance style about 1500, it was the focus of art and humanist culture in the Split of that time. At time of writing, the museum is under renovation.

Accommodation
Hotel Marjan (A category – tel: (058) 42-866, 598 beds) is a modern block near the harbour. Smaller and cheaper is **Slavija** (tel: (058) 47-053), centrally situated and with 58 beds. Householders in Split often approach visitors with offers of good-value accommodation in their homes.
The leafy but unexciting Kastela Riviera to the west, once part of a fortification system, is a convenient dormitory, with various beaches.

Entertainment
The informal pageant of the *korso* promenade passes through Narodni Trg, Split's version of Venice's Piazza San Marco, in continuous chattering flow, of an evening. On Saturday nights a mid-square platform is the stage for entertainments and various bands – anything from vintage Gigli ballads through Country 'n' Western to Hip-Hop – with peripheral dancing. Split has a noted live-arts Summer Festival, as well as a Popular Song Festival.

Excursions
Many scenic places surround the town – the wooded **Marjan Hill** with its lovely views, where Diocletian hunted; **Sustjepan** with its romantic reef covered by fir trees and cypresses; the lidos of **Bačvice** and **Znanj;** the scattered ruins of Roman **Salona;** nearby **Trogir, Kašteli, Omiš;** and the islands of **Šolta, Brač, Hvar, Korčula** and **Vis,** visitable by regular ferries.

Information: Turist Biro, Titova Obala 12 (tel: (058) 42-142).

THE ADRIATIC COAST AND ISLANDS

Sveti Stefan: self-contained luxury

◆◆
SVETI STEFAN AND MILOČER
Montenegro (map pages 50-1)
This area is the pride of Yugoslav tourism. Sveti Stefan is a huddle of carefully-converted former fishermen's houses on an islet. It has won a 'Golden Apple' award from the FIJET international travel writers' association.

Transformed in 1950, it has gained a 'high society' image, with world-known names in politics, business and the arts as clients. It is, not surprisingly, an expensive place to stay.
Joined to the mainland by a causeway, Sveti Stefan is a large rock which has sprouted a roughly concentric growth of mushroom-pink stone houses with terracotta roofs – interspersed with trees, pretty little squares, and gardens – plus a church. The swimming pool, on the open-sea side, is a rare 20th-century-style obtrusion outdoors. Two coarse sandy beaches are landward.
On the restaurant terrace of the de luxe category Villa No 118, guests can sip the house's very special own-label grape brandy.
The accommodations have congenial ambience, with hand-made furniture and embroideries. (Further details after Miločer, below.)

Miločer
In a beautiful setting on the mainland coast facing Sveti Stefan, this verdant and rock-girt village boasts a former royal summer residence converted into a hotel (see below). Its fine-shingle beach slopes serenely into an aquamarine-to-royal-blue sea for safe bathing.

THE ADRIATIC COAST AND ISLANDS

Accommodation
Miločer Hotel (A category). The 50-bed hotel is a low white building, with a gracious vine-roofed terrace, surrounded by 44 acres (18 hectares) of parkland. Its configuration unfortunately makes it not very suitable for the disabled.
More democratically-priced hotels are the **Vila Miločer** (A category, inside the park, and with 120 beds) and the modern **Maestral** (A category, with 294 beds, by the village).
The three hotels above, and the 36 houses plus the luxury category villa in Sveti Stefan, are all run by the same management: Sveti Stefan Hotels, 85315 Sveti Stefan (tel: (086) 41-411 and (086) 41-333). Private householders let out accommodation in Miločer and on nearby slopes.

Excursions
You can take a trip to **Dubrovnik, Boka Kotorska, Cetinje, Ulcinj, Medjugorje** and **Mostar**; or try a local **Fish Picnic**.

Petrovac
Pleasant, but less exclusive, is Petrovac, six miles (10km) further south, another peaceful swim-and-sunbathe place. Above the sandy cove is a medieval fortress, now a nightclub. All around are pine and olive groves. There are minor monasteries in the area.
It has several hotels, the best being the **Palas** (A category – tel: (086) 61-074), with 185 rooms, indoor/outdoor swimming pools. The Autocamp is one of the biggest on the Montenegrin coast.

Trogir's magnificent cathedral

◆◆◆
TROGIR
Croatia (map pages 44-5)
This beautiful town is on an island linked by a bridge to the mainland, 17 miles (27km) west of Split.
The sun shines warmly on its maze of narrow, yellow limestone streets, and there is sometimes a smell of seaweed and new wine.
With a history dating back to the Illyrians, Greeks and Romans, it has preserved many medieval features, especially Romanesque, including palaces, monasteries, a castle and works of art.
The first settlers here were members of a Doric Greek tribe living on the island of Issa (today Vis). Kairos, their portable god of good fortune, guided them to a little off-shore islet which they called

THE ADRIATIC COAST AND ISLANDS

Tragurion ('goat-town'), probably because of the large number of goats in the region. Kairos has remained in Trogir to the present day – as a bas relief in a small museum at the 11th-century **Benedictine convent** of Sveti Nikola.

A local sculptor, Radovan, created works equal to the finest medieval achievements anywhere in Europe. Around the famous portal of the imposing **cathedral** his amazing stone figures seem as clearly defined as when they were carved by the master craftsman in 1240 – two lions, statues of Adam and Eve, various saints, and scenes featuring animals and flowers.

The main square (Narodni Trg) is a showpiece of fine historic buildings.

Accommodation
Hotel Medena (tel: (058) 73-788, 1,380 beds) and **Medena Apartments** (tel: (058) 73-222, 1,142 beds) are both B category. Situated among pine trees, 3½ miles (5.5km) from Trogir, neither is suitable for disabled visitors. Pebbly and rocky beach with man-made sunbathing area.

◆◆
ULCINJ
Montenegro (map pages 50-1)
Ulcinj is the nearest 'family' resort to the Albanian border. Claiming 217 sunny days annually, it has the Yugoslav rarity of *sand* beaches. One beach is said to have proved helpful in rheumatic problems and, via a sulphurous spring, fertility in women. Sandy Velika Plaža (Long Beach), about 2½ miles (4km) south of the town extends 7½ miles (12km) beyond its hotels to the border, and is backed partly by marshland haunts of wild geese, ducks, partridges and game shoots.

During at least one of the three centuries of Turkish rule, ending in 1878, the bigshots locally were the corsairs (and their cannons), who came here from Morocco and Algeria to help the Turks harass the Venetian navy. Even today, some of the oriental garb in the vegetable market may seem to contain North African hues.

In the old, walled town centre is a **prince's palace,** the **Balšić tower,** and an oriental ensemble with the 17th-century **Pasha's mosque,** all much damaged in the 1979 earthquake. On a hill above Ulcinj is **Stari Grad** fortress, mostly ruined.

Great tracts of seaside salt basins are strangely attractive. Around May, seawater is let into the basins and in September, the salt is 'harvested'.

Accommodation
Hotel Grand Lido (B category – tel: (085) 81-033, 112 beds), at Velika Plaža, has various sports facilities.
Hotel Galeb (A category – tel: (085) 81-311, 390 beds), a new hotel on a rocky point, has many amenities but is unsuitable for disabled visitors having numerous steps down to sea-level.
Hotel Otrant (A category – tel: (085) 81-161, 274 beds) is at Velika Plaža and is well equipped. Near by are the new **Villas Otrant** with 260 beds.

THE ADRIATIC COAST AND ISLANDS

Nearby Resorts
Bar. With a car ferry to Bari in Italy, a ferry service to the Greek mainland and Corfu, and a rail link to Beograd, Bar is a transit point and a working town. It has a large port and marina, sandy beach, and plantations of citrus and olive trees in the vicinity. About two miles (3km) inland are the ruins of Stari (old) Bar, an atmospheric site. The original town was brought down in skirmishes between the Montenegrins and Turks in the last century. It comprises quite extensive ruins including several churches, a medieval palace and aqueduct – now much overgrown.
Sutomore, six miles (9.5km) further north, is a hamlet, mainly 19th and 20th century, with a long sandy and pebbly beach for very pleasant bathing, and a scrub-covered rock hinterland becoming mountainous in various directions.

The 12th-century Sveta Tekla church is an example of religious tolerance – Catholic and Orthodox altars side by side, and both still in use, presumably at different times. Two ruined Turkish fortresses seem also to strike a compromise with their names – Haj and Nehaj (Fear and Fear Not).
Accommodation. There are hotels and villas all along the beach at Sutomore. Recommended is the B category **Inex Zlatana Obala** complex (tel: (085) 22-422, 850 beds).

◆
UMAG
Croatia (map pages 50-1)
On a rather less picturesque peninsula than Novigrad's to the south (see page 46), Umag has developed north along an indented coastline with hotels

Traditional fish-traps near Ulcinj

THE ADRIATIC COAST AND ISLANDS

and some attractive 'pavilions' and chalets, which have their own gardens in well-wooded parkland by rocky, man-made or pebbly beaches.

Peaceful tourist settlements, including **Katoro** and **Kanegra,** occupy sites up to five miles (8km) from Umag, reached for some by a mini-train. Various sports and recreations are on hand. The **Za-Za Entertainment Centre** offers programmes for young and old, and there are speciality restaurants.

The modern **Hotel Punta** (B category – tel: (053) 51-482, 512 beds) is nicely designed to appeal to most tastes, set amid trees about a mile (1.5km) from Umag.

Popular excursions are to: **Savudrija,** a fishermen's village and resort to the north; **Buje,** an old hilltop town eight miles (13km) away; **Groznjan,** an artists' colony 12 miles (19km) away; and wine festivals.

Motovun

Best of all is the excursion to medieval Motovun, 24 miles (39km) inland from Umag. Well worth a visit, if not by too many all at once, this hilltop town has remained undisturbed within its medieval fortified walls, with its very steep cobbled streets and elements of 13th-century Venetian, Romanesque, Gothic and Renaissance architecture. Developed from the 10th century, it has an almost-Andalusian distant aspect, and affords most appealing views from its eyrie.

Motovun boasts one hotel (the **Kastel,** B category with 60 beds tel: (053) 81-652).

♦♦ VIS

Croatia (map pages 44-5)
One of the remoter and lovelier Adriatic islands, well worth the leisurely two-hour ferry cruise from Split (daily services in summer) for a visit, Vis has again been opened up to international tourism after a period until 1989, when foreigners could visit only with a special permit, as the island was used for military manoeuvres. During World War II it accommodated the Supreme Headquarters of the National Liberation Army, and the mountain cave containing Marshal Tito's command offices is now a museum.

The town museum, **Memorijalni Muzej Vojne Skole Nov, Poj i Nkoj,** contains World War II militaria, as well as more ancient relics.

Open: daily (except Monday) 09.00-12.00 and 17.00-19.00 hrs.

Eating Out

Sea-bass and other fish are tastily prepared for alfresco suppers at a restaurant or two around the romantic waterfront. The island's central plain raises grapes for the excellent deep red *Vugava* wine, a muscatel, and other white varieties.

Excursions

Komiza is a small, pretty port on the west coast, with a splendid keep, a Benedictine monastery, monumental churches, and a particularly good restaurant on the broad quayside.

From here, boat excursions can be made to the out-island of **Biševo,** with its steep caverned cliffs and 'Blue Grotto'.

THE ADRIATIC COAST AND ISLANDS

♦♦
VRSAR
Croatia (map pages 50-1)
Around the north bank of the Limska Kanal (Lim Fjord) inlet, Vrsar presents a classic Mediterranean panorama of arcades and rooftops in static cascade down to the Romanesque basilica and fishermen's cottages in the port. Among notable sights are a mosaic from the 4th century, a basilica from the 12th, and an artists' foundation established near Vrsar by the sculptor, Džamonja. A cruise round the beautiful Limska Kanal can be made by ketch from Poreč.

The restaurant **Gostiona Vrsar** restores the inner person with platters of pork chops, liver, beef, kebab and salads, with local wines, at philanthropic prices.

Accommodation
This includes several B category hotels, with little to choose between them, on tree-fringed sites with man-made sunbathing beaches, separated by a short walk from the town. There is also the pleasant family and children-orientated **Holiday Village Petalon** (B category – tel: (053) 41-198, 186 beds), and its apartments about 1¼ miles (2km) south in a bay near the enormous **Koversada Naturist Centre** (international repute). **Funtana,** by Limska Kanal, means 'Fountain'. It remains a fairly typical seaside village, with the addition of a hotel, **Funtana** (B category – tel: (053) 41-511, 464 beds), and campsite accommodation.

♦♦♦
ZADAR
Croatia (map pages 44-5)
The ancient capital of Dalmatia, Zadar concentrates its interesting sights in a small peninsula, where traffic is confined to a perimeter road. Almost every house has historical significance.
The town's hinterland lost many monuments in 72 bombing raids in World War II, but the peninsula escaped much damage. Its round pre-Romanesque **Sveti Donat** (St Donatus) church, from the 9th century, incorporates stones from the Roman forum on which it is sited. There is a Romanesque **cathedral**, and other medieval churches. There are Renaissance and baroque palaces and the beautiful **Land Gate** of 1543.
Museums, a large flea-market and a yacht marina are among other features. Tavernas serve speciality grills, and their Maraskino cherry brandy is made locally.

Accommodation
By shingly beaches in the piney outlying settlement of Zadar-Borik are several modern B category hotels and apartments used by tour operators. Further information might be obtained through the **Hotel Barbara** (A category – tel: (057) 24-299).

Excursions
Trips can be made to nearby **Ugljan** and **Pašman** islands and, a little further, to the strange and beautiful **Kornat** archipelago.

THE NORTH

Timeless peace lies over Lake Bled

THE NORTH

Slovenia's lakes and mountains are the main attraction of inland northern Yugoslavia. Winter sports, though less developed than in the older skiing areas of Austria and Switzerland, are increasingly popular, and the scenery is a draw for summer visitors. The caves of Postojna and Škocjan are among Europe's most spectacular systems; and for more sophisticated pleasures there are the Slovenian and Croatian capitals Ljubljana and Zagreb.

What to See

◆◆◆
BLED
Slovenia

With year-round appeal – as shimmering trout lake, spa, walking centre or handy base for skiing – Bled has been a scenic resort since well before this century. Some of its more gracious period buildings testify to this, though not all its newer accommodations harmonise happily in style with these. Once a haunt of royalty, the Hotel Vila Bled (see page 68) was more recently a summer residence of the late President Tito.

You may still hear the gentle clip-clop of patient horses pulling landaus round the tree-fringed shore, and there is little motorboat noise to drown the chiming of the bell of **Sveta Marija**, a church now converted to a museum, on an islet in the middle of the lake.

Open: daily 08.00-20.00 hrs (closes earlier in winter).

In exhilarating alpine air, there is golf at an 18-hole course, and from almost everywhere, there are breath-catching views of mountains, forest and lake.

In summer, Bled seems to attract the more mature, but all age-groups enjoy romantic dining out on lakeside terraces, and there are discos as well as the Casino Hall with its dancing to live music.

THE NORTH

Accommodation
The A category **Grand Hotel Toplice** (tel: (064) 77-222, 205 beds) enjoys a thermal spa-water supply, and a particularly good reputation for food.
Vila Bled (A category – tel: (064) 77-436). Rather exclusive, with only 64 beds (see page 67). There are hotels and pensions in most categories, not all being on the lakeshore itself, and they are generally of good standard.

Excursions
Destinations can include the **Lipica** horse stud, **Postojna Caves** and **Venice**.

Skiing
This is mainly at **Zatrnik**, reached in a 15-minute ski-bus journey which is free for lift-pass holders. There, with a 4,170-foot (1,271m) top station, the 16 *pistes* are most attractive to beginners and intermediates. Advanced performers can try the slalom, which has featured in the European Cup.

◆◆◆ BOHINJSKO JEZERO
Slovenia
In its beautiful wooded valley in Nacionalni Park Triglav (Triglav Alpine National Park), 20 miles (32km) from Bled, this clean blue glacial lake with adjacent mountains is attractive in summer as well as in the skiing season.
Rowing, angling, cycling, hiking, hunting and mountaineering are among available activities.
Sightseeing can include the nearby **Savica Slap** (Savica Falls), **Hudicev Most** (the Devil's Bridge) on the River Mostnica, the 9,395-foot (2,863m) peak of **Mount Triglav** (Yugoslavia's highest) and the stunning panorama from the cable car station on **Mount Vogel**.

Skiing
Skiing here, both alpine and

The mirror of glacial Lake Bohinj

THE NORTH

cross-country, offers plenty of scope. Of the two alpine centres, **Vogel** is the more lively and attractive, with a season from November to May.

From the lake, the cable car ascends to the 5,046-foot (1,538m) starting point for two chair and three drag lifts, with access to runs for all types of skier and good snow from mid-December to mid-April. A special attraction, with very demanding slopes that are certainly not for beginners, is the 5¼ mile (8.5km) run from the 6,230-foot (1,899m) top station down to the lake.

At the very beginning of the Vogel slopes is the **Ski-Hotel Vogel**, C category, and not highly recommended.

Kobla is a quiet resort area, nicely built and maintained. Runs go from 4,935 feet (1,504m), and the most important is the 3½ mile (6km) 'family run'. There are three chair lifts and three drags. From Kobla there are cross-country trails, and there is one from nearby Rudno Polje to Bohinjska Bistrica.

Accommodation

Among the best of 11 hotels and pensions in Bohinjsko Jezero are the **Kompas** (B category – tel: (064) 723-471, 123 beds) with summer outdoor swimming pool, and sports grounds; and the **Zlatorog**, (B category – tel: (064) 723-384, 96 beds), with indoor swimming pool. There are numerous mountain houses (quite far from the lake) and private rooms are also usually available.

General Information: Turistbiro Bohinj (tel: (064) 76-370).

◆◆
BOVEC AND KOBARID
Slovenia

In a magnificent alpine valley setting, southwest across the Vršič pass from Kranjska Gora, **Bovec** already has a burgeoning reputation with intermediate and advanced skiers on its 8,481-foot (2,585m) Mount Kanin. Now it is attracting summer visitors with kayaking instruction on the River Soča, fishing, and walking.

Good snow has been reported from Bovec's 7,221-foot (2,201m) top station when this has been absent from other European resorts in December and January. However, this is not an ideal resort for beginners' enjoyment.

The B category **Hotel Kanin** (tel: (065) 86-021, 240 beds), is a well-equipped skiers' hotel.

Kobarid, to the southeast, is a small town known for a World War I battle (Caporetto). Its houses attractively mix alpine and Mediterranean types of architecture.

◆◆
KRANJSKA GORA
Slovenia

Winter sports are Kranjska Gora's best-known attractions internationally. Set between the Karavanke mountains and Julian Alps near the borders with Austria and Italy, it was a typical traditional alpine village until accommodation requirements brought about a slightly strange architectural admixture. (Older buildings include the 16th-century church of St Mary's Assumption, and a chapel built by World War I Russian

THE NORTH

The ski resort of Kranjska Gora

prisoners by the highland road to Vršič.)
Skiing is possible from late November to early May, but the season proper is December–April. Ski-runs up to 7,645 feet (2,330m) meet a range of abilities from beginners' to World cup competitors' and 19 miles (30km) of prepared *pistes* are augmented by a 28-mile (45km) cross-country course. Near by is the famous ski jump at Planica.
Near Kranjska Gora village, with its ski shop and ski rental, two nursery slopes and four runs for beginners are served by six of the 19 ski lifts. The ski school takes children aged from seven upwards, though lessons can be arranged for under-sevens. Beginners can progress to the wooded slopes of Mount Vitranc or the ski school run by the

Yugoslav world champion, Bojan Krisaj, at Gozd Martuljak.
For intermediates, Kranjska Gora offers an interesting diversity of well-marked red runs, and a system of chair and drag lifts.
There are horse-drawn sleigh rides, and *après-ski* includes fondue and pizza parties, discos, night-clubs, bars, swimming (in three hotels) or sauna.
Summer visitors to Kranjska Gora and the adjoining national park around Mount Triglav, Yugoslavia's highest peak (9,393 feet/2,863m), can enjoy scenic walking, climbing, fishing, botany, pot-holing and canoeing. Slovenia's beautiful lakes are within easy reach.

Accommodation

Sample hotels: **Kompas** (A category – tel: (064) 88-661), with 300 beds, café, bar, restaurant, swimming pool, tennis, table tennis, bowling, sauna; **Lek** (B category – tel: (064) 88-520), more intimate with 140 beds, but similar facilities to Kompas, plus children's playground. Accommodation also includes pensions and village rooms.

General Information: Turistično Društvo Kranjska Gora (tel: (064) 88-768).

◆
LIPICA
Slovenia
The Lipica stud-farm, near Slovenia's Italian border, has a 400-year-old tradition of raising thoroughbred Lipizzaner horses. The stud was founded in 1580 by the Austrian archduke Karl, son of the emperor Ferdinand,

when a lighter, more elegant horse was demanded by the nobility.
There are 60 horses available for recreational riding, riding courses for both beginners and advanced riders, and for dressage. There is a highly qualified team of instructors. Non-riding guests can enjoy carriage rides, and children can take daily pony rides.
The climax of a day visit to Lipica is the exhibition performance by the classical riding school with their specially-trained horses.

Accommodation
The light and airy, modern traditional-style **Hotel Maestoso** (named after a famous Lipizzaner stallion) is B category with 142 beds (tel: (067) 73-541).
Klub Hotel Lipica (B category – tel: (067) 73-597, 163 beds) is another possibility.

Excursions
Places worth excursion visits are the **Škocjan** and **Vilenica** caves, the medieval villages of **Štanjel** and **Lokev**, and the Istrian coastal resorts.

◆◆
LJUBLJANA
Slovenia
This characteristic capital city of independently-minded Slovenia, in a green plain surrounded by hills, almost looks like a collection of film sets for some Austro-Hungarian period epic.
Ljubljana has managed to preserve some relics from its Roman past, its three romantic bridges across the River Ljubljanica, the original town centre and its three squares, Renaissance and baroque façades, embellished portals, uneven roofs, and narrow streets.
A craze to keep up with 1960s international high-rise trends has produced some featureless modern blocks. But conservationist views have since come into fashion to check such obtrusions into dignified streets. Noise pollution is apparently a problem which cannot easily be addressed.
Some old town streets by what is spiritually the Left Bank of the Ljubljanica have little motorised traffic, and tend, in summer, to be partially covered with café-bar tables, occupied mostly by earnestly-debating young university students.
Facing Prešernov Trg (Prešeren Square) is the 17th-century **Frančiskanska Cerkev** (Franciscan church and abbey), built in 1646, with its majestic great altar of 1738, the work of Francesco Robba.
Crossing Tromostovje (Three Bridges) the path leads to **Ljubljana Rotovž** or Town Hall, built in the second half of the 15th century and frequently restored, particularly after the severe earthquake of 1895. The famous **Robba Fountain**, in front of the town hall, is an allegory of the three rivers, the Sava, Ljubljanica and Krka, and is one of the most beautiful baroque monuments in Slovenia.
The early 18th-century **Ljubljana Cathedral** (Sveti Nikola) and the Bishop's Palace are in Ciril Metodov Trg (Cyril-Methodius Square). The cathedral was begun in 1700, with the *trompe*

THE NORTH

l'oeil painting of the ceiling and interior entrusted to the Italian painter Julio Quaglia.
The **Ljubljana Seminary,** next to the Cathedral, has a majestic portal, with giants. Its baroque Library contains a fine collection of medieval manuscripts.
Mestni Trg (City Square) is old Ljubljana's third square.
The origin of **Ljubljana Grad** (castle) is not known. Although a fortified station probably stood here in prehistoric and Roman times, the castle is documented only from the 15th century. The most recent reconstruction began in 1968 and continues. There are several museums of limited interest. The **Narodni Muzej** (National Museum), Trg Herajev 1, is notable for its extravagant staircase.
Open: daily (except Monday) 10.00-18.00 hrs (Sunday until 13.00 hrs).

Accommodation

Holiday Inn (luxury class – tel: (061) 211-434) has 196 beds and many facilities.
Hotel Slon (B category – tel: (061) 211-232) has 259 beds.

Entertainment and Nightlife

The International Summer Festival (concerts, jazz festival, wine fair, etc) is a favourite attraction, and there is sometimes a 'country wedding festival' in the surrounding area (see pages 101 and 105). The cafés around Prešernov Trg provide plenty of life in the evening.

Tourist Information Centre:
Titova Cesta 11 (tel: (061) 224-222).

◆◆◆
PLITVIČKA JEZERA (PLITVICE LAKES)
Croatia
In their carefully conserved national park (closed to motorised traffic), the 16 Plitvice Lakes successively overflow and cascade down into each other along five miles (8km) of forest and rocky gorge by means of a series of waterfalls, the highest being 260 feet (79m). The lakes are also linked by systems of caves and underground channels.
Along with the spring-fed water's mineral content, algae or mosses help to give the lakes attractive shades of green-to-blue (and there are theories that waterfalls make for healthier fresh air by increasing its proportion of negative ions, as does an ioniser).
The rustic-style hotels near the biggest lake, Kozjak, serve a nature resort area with 50 miles (80km) of walkways (see page 91). In high summer it may be cooler than some regions, and in autumn the beeches and other deciduous trees among the conifers provide further colour.
Plitvice Lakes comprise a UNESCO-recognised institution attracting nearly a million sightseers a year, and with plenty of room for them to find solitude amid woods and waters.

Accommodation
Hotels include the A category **Jezero** (tel: (048) 76-316) with 486 beds and **Plitvice** (tel: (048) 76-522) with 150 beds, and the B category **Bellevue** (tel: (048) 76-344) with 189 beds.

THE NORTH

One of Plitvice's mighty waterfalls

♦♦♦
POSTOJNSKA JAMA (POSTOJNA CAVES)
Slovenia

These are some of the world's most beautiful underground caverns. One special feature is their size – their magnificent galleries, total 16½ miles (27km) in length.

Parts of the caves are toured by electric railway which takes in illuminated halls, abysses, fantastic stalactites and stalagmites, and underground streams. **Pivka Jama** and the **Črna** (Black) **Jama** are part of the Postojna Caves system and are well worth visiting. They are entered from the large Pivka Jama campsite, which includes bungalows, restaurants and sports grounds (tel: (067) 21-382). *Caves open:* for conducted tours, daily. From April to October tours run on the half-hour or hour from 08.30-18.00 hrs (last tour in April and October at 17.00hrs); November to March, tours are at 09.30 and 13.30 hrs, with additonal tours at 11.30 and 15.00 hrs at weekends.

Prejkamski Grad (the Castle of Predjama), perched in the middle of a high perpendicular cliff, is 5½ miles (9km) from Postojna. It was built in 1570 and houses an interesting permanent exhibition, including palaeolithic finds, old weapons and furniture and the remains of the Partisan printing-office.

Northeast of Postojna is the wild gorge, **Rakov Škocjan**, a national park, and periodic **Cerkniško Jezero** (Cerknica Lake).

Accommodation

In B category are hotels **Jama** (tel: (067) 21-172, 305 beds) and **Kras** (tel: (067) 21-071, 108 beds). The **Motel Proteus** (tel: (067) 21-250) has 486 beds.

THE NORTH

♦♦♦
ŠKOCJANSKE JAME (ŠKOCJAN CAVES)
Slovenia

Less famous than Postojna, Škocjan caves lie eight miles (13km) from Lipica and extend for about three miles (5km), about 1½ miles (2.3km) of which are accessible to the public.

THE NORTH

They are entered by an elevator, have electric lighting, and tours take place six times a week during the season, three times out of season.

A guided walk lasts two hours (guides speak at least five languages), taking in a wild, underground world, pools, and gigantic stalagmites.
The impressive **Velika Dvorana** (Great Hall) has a collection of imposing stalagmites. Daylight streams into the enormous **Schmidl's Hall,** and **Velika Dolina** (Big Valley) has a 535-foot (163m) waterfall cascading into a lake.
For information on tours, telephone (067) 74-548.

◆◆ ZAGREB
Croatia

Thrustful capital of westward-orientated Croatia and second largest city in the country, Zagreb has long been the biggest trade and industrial town of Yugoslavia and a major international transit point. It is also an important centre of culture, education, and tourism. Though Zagreb overlooks the green plain of the River Sava, there are slightly alpine outlines in the wide-eaved farms and prosperous-looking suburban villas passed on the road from the airport into town, where high-rise apartments, hotels, and the modern facilities of the trade fair site reflect a busy commercial scene. To the north of the city lie the unspoilt hills and valleys of Zagorje.
Settlements existed hereabouts from palaeolithic times, with a Roman town (Andautonia) on the site until the 6th century AD. First written records are from 1094, when Zagreb's bishopric citadel (Kaptol) was founded. Some of its walls survive, but

THE NORTH

invading Tartars were characteristically destructive in the 13th century. The parallel lay medieval town of Gradec was built, eventually, as Gornji Grad (Upper Town), to merge with Kaptol to form Zagreb in the 1850s, along with the newer – and still growing – Donji Grad (Lower Town).

Sightseeing

The 13th-century **Cathedral** in Zagreb's Kaptol district, was several times rebuilt to become, in its present 19th-century form, the loftiest in Yugoslavia with twin bell towers and spires. The old Gradec sector has a special atmosphere around its baroque and classical palaces, churches, monasteries and houses. **Sveti Marko** (St Mark's) church is mainly Gothic, from the 14th century, but features some fine modern work, including sculptures by Meštrović. Also in Gradec, the 17th-century Jesuit Monastery has been adapted into a fine Arts Centre.

The Lower Town was created by the architect Milan Lenuci, after the earthquake of 1880. Donji Grad's squares, parks and monuments create a pleasant impression. Highlights include Ilica (the shopping street), Trg Republike (Republic Square), and the big food produce market between this square and the Kaptol.

Museums include the **Galerija Primitivne Umietnosti (Naivne)** (Gallery of Primitive Art), Ćirilmetodska 3 (*open:* daily 10.00-13.00 hrs and 17.00-18.00 hrs, Sunday 10.00-13.00 hrs); the **Etnografski Muzej** (Ethnographic Museum), Mažuranićev Trg 14, with a good collection of Croatian costume (*open:* daily, except Monday, 09.00-15.00 hrs, Saturday and Sunday 09.00-13.00 hrs); and the **Strossmayerova Galerija Starih Majstora** (Strossmayer Gallery), Trg Nikole Subića Zrinskog 11 (*open:* daily (except Monday) 10.00-13.00 hrs, also Tuesday 17.00-19.00 hrs) – Yugoslavia's largest collection of Old Masters.

Accommodation

Since the Universiade events of 1987, hotels have been improved in quality and quantity. One of the best anywhere is the A category **Esplanade** (tel: (041) 435-666, 370 beds). It is near the railway station, its sound-proofing probably now improved on that side, and its updated facilities have not marred its ambience of old-style luxury. The capacious and somewhat clinical B category **Hotel International** (tel: (041) 511-511), in a less convenient modern district, caters well but rather impersonally for transit visitors – not without traffic noise being audible in some bedrooms (600 beds).

Entertainment

Night-clubs thrive. Jazz is alive and well. For serious music lovers, musical institutions include I Solisti Zagreb chamber orchestra.

General Information. Of several Tourist Information centres in the city, the main one is at Trg Nikole Zrinjskog 14 (tel: (041) 411-883).

THE SOUTH

THE SOUTH

Inland Montenegro and Macedonia and southern Serbia, with the troubled autonomous region of Kosovo, are still largely off the main tourist track. Yet there is much of interest there, including Orthodox monasteries with fine frescos; the inland lakes of Ohrid, Prespa and Skadar; and skiing in the mountains.

What to See

◆◆
BITOLA
Macedonia
The second town of Macedonia, once famous for tobacco, is of interest mainly for the archaeological site of **Heraclea Lyncestis,** two miles (3km) outside it. Probably founded by Philip II of Macedon (father of Alexander the Great), its main glory is the fine mosaic floors with Hellenistic and Early Christian designs. Well preserved Roman baths, an amphitheatre and two basilicas are among the buildings excavated, and it is thought these are just a fraction of the whole city.
Open: daily 09.00-19.00 hrs.

◆◆◆
CETINJE
Montenegro
Capital of Montenegro from 1482 to 1945, and seat of its last independent ruler, King Nikola 1, idiosyncratic Cetinje has a wealth of remarkable 19th-century buildings that include former embassies and legations of major powers.
About 45 minutes' drive up from

Heraclea Lyncestis: floor mosaic

coastal Budva, it is at the foot of Mount Lovćen, on whose peak is the mausoleum of Petar Petrović Njegoš II, the revered prince-bishop and poet, who died in 1851.
Njegoš's palace in Cetinje, a squat two-storeyed building, is called the **Biljarda** because it still contains a billiard table imported by him at great expense and effort when it was a nationally unique curiosity. Its three museums also house furniture, portraits, ethnographic items and literature – some of which he wrote himself.
Next to Biljarda there is a huge relief **map of Montenegro** made by Austrian soldiers in 1917. Behind it is Sveti Petar Monastery, completed in 1701 by Danilo, founder of the Njegoš dynasty. Here, among the treasury's 15th- and 16th-century icons and religious books, is the gospel known as *The Octoih of the First Voice*. One of the oldest printed books in

THE SOUTH

existence, post-dating Caxton's *Histories of Troy* by only 18 years, it was published in 1493.
Open: daily, 08.00-19.00 hrs April to October, 09.00-17.00 hrs the rest of the year.
In a park opposite the Biljarda is the **Muzej Cetinje** (State Museum), Titov Trg, which was the palace of King Nikola 1, also visitable on a guided tour, and displaying various possessions of the monarch.
Open: daily 09.00-19.00 hrs in season.

Accommodation
Grand Hotel (A category – tel: (086) 21-144, 420 beds) is the only listed hotel. Private rooms are negotiable from owners who sometimes wait at the bus station, or from details at the tourist office – **Turistički Savez Opatine,** Ulica Bajova 2 (tel: (086) 21-395).

Remote Lake Dojran

◆
DOJRANSKO EZERO (LAKE DOJRAN)
Macedonia
Fishing with the aid of cormorants and other birds is the fascinating tradition carried on here in autumn and winter. Attracted on to the lake to feed, these birds chase the fish into channelled traps among reeds and canes, where they are netted, under cane-thatched 'hides' on stilts in the water.
Of the lake's 26½ square-mile (43sq km) surface, 16½ square miles (27sq km) are in Macedonia and the rest in Greece.
Private rooms accommodation is available in Stari Dojran, in addition to the **Hotel Polin** (B category – tel: (093) 83-713), 122 beds), and the **Hotel Galeb** (B category – tel: (093) 83-707).

General Information: Turističko Društvo, 91487 Stari Dojran.

THE SOUTH

Žabljak, Yugoslavia's highest town

♦♦♦
DURMITOR SINJAVINA
Montenegro

The Durmitor massif is largely a national park offering a sensational diversity of landscapes, and entered on UNESCO's World Heritage List (see also page 96). It is bounded by canyons of two of Yugoslavia's wildest rivers, the Piva and Tara.

The Tara Gorge is said to be second only in depth to America's Grand Canyon. It is on the international Biosphere Reserve list. Whitewater rafting is organised along its rushing river, with its sporadic rapids. The mountain (highest peak Bobotov Kuk, 8,275 feet/2,522m) is patterned with forests, 22 glacier lakes, peaceful pastures, brilliant summer flowers, awesome chasms, gentler creeks, caves, barren 'moonscapes', and sweeping views of snowy peaks – even in summer.

Crno Jezero (Black Lake), two miles (3km) from the summer and winter resort of Žabljak (see below) by asphalted road, is widely regarded as *the* natural beauty of the area. With a dark greenish colour, it resembles a long figure-eight in shape and is probably the result of two lakes merging. A phenomenon around May is the annual 'explosion' of water gushing down into it from the swollen Celina spring, on a rocky slope above the lake.

The area also has dramatic World War II associations. Here, Tito and his Partisans were joined by one of the first British liaison parties, parachuted in.

Žabljak

The highest town in Yugoslavia, at 4,806 feet (1,465m), Žabljak has developed in recent years from a quaint collection of wooden houses into a friendly summer and winter resort sporting modern hotels, shops, restaurants, hospital, National Park management and civic offices.

Accommodation

Among hotels are the **Jezera** (B category – tel: (0872) 88-226, with villas and apartments for

THE SOUTH

Winter playground, Kopaonik

rental) and the **Planinka** (B category – tel: (0872) 88-344).

General Information: Nacionalni Park Durmitor, 87220 Žabljak, tel: (0872) 88-346.

◆
KOPAONIK
Serbia
Purpose-built, in splendid natural surroundings, Kopaonik is considered to provide the best skiing and facilities in eastern and central Yugoslavia. At 5,315–5,807 feet (1,620–1,770m) amid smoothly-contoured uplands, it has 27 miles (44km) of wide and ably maintained *pistes* with 20 interconnecting chairlifts and drags serving up to 13,500 skiers per hour.

Floodlit night skiing is a regular feature near the apartment settlement, which has a cosily traditional atmosphere despite its being relatively new, and has a congenial selection of restaurants, cafés and bars. *Après-ski* is lively.

For summer visitors there are numerous and varied walks, and guided tours to historic monasteries, character towns and metropolitan Beograd.

Accommodation
Grand Hotel Karavan (B category – tel: (036) 71-034, 431 beds).
Bačiste (B category – tel: (036) 71-023, 236 beds).
Apartments Konaci Sunčani Vrhovi (tel: (036) 71-029, 1,300 beds).

◆
NIŠ
Serbia
The second largest town in Serbia, industrial Niš is not an obvious tourist attraction. However, its longstanding reputation as a gateway between east and west is perceptible both in its historical and modern features.

Čele-Kula (the tower of skulls) on Brace Taškovica, was built by Turks with the macabre structural incorporation of over 950 skulls of Serbians who blew themselves up in defiance when besieged in the battle of Čegar (1809). Even Lord Byron was daunted by this spectacle. Today, 60 skulls remain in the tower walls, within a protective enclosure.
Open: Monday to Saturday 09.00-16.00 hrs, Sunday 10.00-14.00 hrs.

To the east, by the road to Niška Spa, are traces of Roman Mediana.

The **Tvrdjava** (or Istanbul Gate Fortress) is located across the Nišava river, opposite Liberation Square, which has a row of well-preserved 19th-

THE SOUTH

century Balkan-style houses. The present fortress dates from the early 18th century.
There is a produce/'flea'-market by the Fortress Wall to add colour to an indifferent city centre scene. Restaurants serve esteemed spicy food.
Hotels include the B category **Ambassaor** (tel: (018) 25-650, 306 beds), in the centre.

General Information:
Srbija-Turist Agency, Voždova 12, Niš (tel: (018) 25-249).

♦♦♦
NOVI PAZAR
Serbia
Once an important town on the trade route between the Adriatic and Istanbul, Novi Pazar still has its Turkish quarter and is on the tourist itineraries for its lively market (best on Tuesdays), which will appeal more to those who like local colour than to souvenir-hunters.
Two extremely important medieval monasteries are accessible from here. **Sopoćani,** 10 miles (16km) west, was built as his mausoleum by the Nemanjić King Uroš I in about 1260. The fine and unusually large frescos have been excellently restored.
Studenica, about 30 miles (48km) north of Novi Pazar, is Serbia's richest monastery complex with three churches (out of an original seven), and other buildings.
The medieval King Stefan 1 was crowned at Studenica. There are some particularly fine frescos surviving from the 13th century, though most are from later periods. At one time the monks ran a very early hospital and research school for mental diseases – apparently similar to today's ills. During the feuds between resistance fighters in World War II, opposing sides would both seek sanctuary here – fortunately, at different times.

Accommodation
The **Vrbak** (A category – tel: (020) 24-844, 130 beds) is the best hotel in Novi Pazar.
In July and August, visitors (up to 12 at a time) can spend a night at Studenica Monastery, when monks will greet them with sweet jam and water, then with their excellent monastery brandy and coffee. Vegetables provided for meals are monastery-grown; food is prepared to old monastic recipes and served with home-made wine.

The 'Birth of the Virgin' from a fresco in Studenica Monastery

THE SOUTH

♦♦♦
OHRID
Macedonia

As one of the oldest lakes in the world – 4 million years – and among the deepest in Europe, **Ohridsko Ezero** boasts several species of fish (including two succulent kinds of trout) and plants which are unknown or long-extinct elsewhere. A third of the 224-square-mile (580sq km) lake is in Albania (shown as Shqipëria on maps). Its attractions to discerning travellers include its colourful translucency down to 70 feet (21m), its panoramic mountain surroundings, the charm of the town of Ohrid, local ecclesiastical art and history, and ancient traditions. Lake and town were entered on UNESCO's List of the World's Natural and Cultural Heritage in 1980.
At 2,200 feet (670m), Ohrid enjoys many hours of balmy sunshine in summer and mild winters, and for visitors there are boat trips, fishing, clean shingle/sand beaches, and the locality's indefinable kind of tranquillity-cum-animation. Ohrid's waterfront main piazza bustles with pleasantly modern, businesslike services, architecturally sympathetic amenities, cafés, bars, restaurants, shops that open from 08.00 to 22.00 hours or so even on Sundays, and trendily dressed young people.

Sightseeing

In a westerly direction, lanes overhung with jettied Balkan houses and Romanesque-tiled eaves lead off in lazy zigzags upwards through the huddle of the old town to its gentle summit, ramparted by the tree-girt remains of Tsar Samuilo's 10th-century fortress. Some of the most striking traditional buildings can be seen after entering low-level Ulica Tsar Samuil, and before commencing any climb. Two of them house the interesting Narodni Muzej (National Museum) about half-way along on the right (*open:* Monday to Friday 07.00–15.00 hrs).
Off to the left towards the end of the street (and roughly opposite the **Sveta Sofija** fish restaurant, with lake eel specialities in spring) is the cathedral church of **Sveta Sofija**. Its rare frescos of Old and New Testament subjects, notably near the altar, date from the 11th to 14th centuries. The church was turned into a mosque by the Turks (note the mimbar, or pulpit), who covered the frescos with whitewash, thus helping to preserve them for future art historians.
Closed: Mondays; opening times vary.
Towards the top of the old town is the church of **Sveti Kliment,** built in 1295. At Ohrid in 893, Sveti Kliment established the first Slavonic university, and more than one church bears his name. This main Sveti Kliment church contains many precious icons, manuscripts from the 10th century and interesting frescos. The latter (restored) cover virtually every square inch of the interior and feature the rare signatures of their late 13th-century creators, Mihajo and Eutihije.
Open: daily (except Mondays) 08.00-12.00 and 15.00-17.00 hrs.

THE SOUTH

Accommodation
Most of the package holiday hotels have their spacious individual settings by the lake and the road which runs south from Ohrid town. If you want to stay in the town, the best bet is private rooms (apply to the Tourist Bureau – see below).

Eating and Shopping
Belvica and *Letnica* are two of the lake's trout species, prepared by restaurants to various local recipes, the latter having pale pink flesh like salmon-trout.
Plasiča are smaller fish whose most-prized features are their scales – transformed by a secret process into 'Ohrid pearls' used in necklaces and other costume jewellery. Wood-carving, candles, and leather-work are among the specialities of souvenir shops.

Entertainment
Old Ohrid is the setting for cultural events, including the Ohrid Summer Festival, centred on the cathedral of Sveta Sofija, in July/August. It is followed by an international poetry festival in neighbouring Struga, near the northernmost point of the lake.

Excursions
Excursions by hydrofoil or small ferry-boat can be made to Peštani and the monastery of **Sveti Naum,** first built by the saint himself around 900AD. On an eminence with views of gently wooded landscape and the grim Albanian border-post, it contains interior paintings. Adjoining its courtyard is a restaurant, open in summer. The monastery of **Sveti Jovan**

Old ways are the norm in Ohrid

Bigorski is in a hillside forest north of Ohrid, about 60 miles (100km) along the beautiful Drim and Radika valleys on the Albanian border. It has remarkably intricate carvings in its iconostasis, and its former refectory still has atmosphere.

General Information: Turističko Biro, Ulica Partizanska.

◆◆
PEĆ
Kosovo
Ethnic Albanians, who are in the majority here, call this historic town Peja, and it is Ipek to the Turks. It is on the edge of the fertile plain of Metohija, near the entrance to a rugged gorge. In the town centre, several walled 18th-century Albanian houses were built with a defensive as well as residential function. Bajrakli Džamija (mosque) is from the 15th

THE SOUTH

century and the Turkish bath from the 16th.

A local pearl is **Pećka Patrijaršija** (Patriarchate of Peć), originally four 13th- and 14th-century churches which were eventually amalgamated. It served as mausoleum for Serbian bishops. There are good frescos from all periods, and the treasury has a collection of sarcophagi, icons and other valuables.

Accommodation

The **Korzo** hotel (tel: (039) 22-423) is B category with 92 beds.

The **Merohija** (A category – tel: (039) 22-424, 152 beds) often serves particularly delicious food in pristine surroundings. Its downstairs toilets can be a put-off.

Excursion

The monastery church of **Dečani**, 13 miles (20km) from Peć, is Serbia's largest. It escaped damage by the Turks unlike most monasteries, and its walls are crammed with hundreds of frescos, including a family tree of the Nemanjić kings of Serbia.

◆
PRESPANSKO EZERO (LAKE PRESPA)
Macedonia

Serene escapism is the summer scene by this high-altitude Macedonian lake.

It is remote and somewhat Arcadian, with deciduous trees and apple orchards below pineclad hills. Villages go about rural business, but there is no sizeable town such as on nearby Lake Ohrid.

Lake fish and game from Mount Galičica can be specialities in tourist restaurants. On the island of Golem Grad are ruins of an old fort and the monastery of Sveti Petar, and in the village of Kurbinovo is the ancient monastery of Sveti Djorje with its remarkable 12th-century frescos.

Accommodation

The two or three hotels – of more recent construction than their stone-and-tile materials may suggest – are in calm wooded settings by the partly-sandy lake shore. They include **Hotel Jugoslavija** (B category – tel: (096) 74-100). There is also the **Krani Campsite.**

◆◆
PRIZREN
Kosovo

This is (and feels) one of the oldest towns in Serbia. It is the nicest in the sometimes-troubled province of Kosovo, with charm and warmth emanating from the old Balkan-style houses in its centre, and picturesque arrangements of dwellings on surrounding hillsides.

In the 7th century BC it was home to the Illyrians. It was named Theranda by the Romans and Prizidijana by the Byzantines. For some time it was capital of the Serbian medieval state, and Turkish rule from 1455 to 1912 left it with much of its appearance today – in fact Turkish is still spoken. In each period it was a major trading and military centre.

On the hill above the town stands the dilapidated fortress

THE SOUTH

Kaljaja – stronghold of the Nemanjić kings in the 13th century.

The large **Sinan Pasha mosque** from 1615, and its tall minaret, stand in the centre of town. Near by is a restored stone bridge dating from the 15th century, crossing the River Bistrica, and the church of **Begorodica Ljeviška** from 1307. With a central dome surrounded by four smaller ones, the church is a typical Serbo-Byzantine edifice. Its frescos are of great value.

Accommodation
The B category **Theranda** (tel: (029) 22-292) with 130 beds (some four to a room) is in the centre of town.

◆
SKADARSKO JEZERO (LAKE SKADAR)
Montenegro
The Balkans' largest lake, also known as Lake Scutari, this

Few visitors venture to see the strange landscape of Lake Skadar

could be a Mecca for naturalists. It attracts more than 260 bird species, including pelicans, and among its 40 species of fish are edible varieties like carp, trout and eels.

Skadarsko Jezero is partly in Albania (Shqipëria). Mainly shallow, with reed-fringed islets and scrub-covered rocks, it has a surface area that can vary from 27 square miles (70 sq km) in summer to 210 square miles (540 sq km) in spring and autumn. Proclaimed a national park (Nacionalni Park Skadarsko Jezero) in 1984, it is surrounded by at least 70 cultural and historical monuments, many from medieval times. A very narrow, often-curving road skirts most of the lake, but it requires care and patience.

On a lake tributary, **Rijeka Crnojevića** was once an important town, known as 'the Venice of Lake Skadar'. It still has a medieval stone bridge which reflects past glories, but its most important feature is

THE SOUTH

probably the small factory which turns out delicious smoked local fish.
The characterful lakeside town of **Virpazar** has one small hotel, the B category **13 Jul** (tel: (085) 71-120). Tourism is not yet much organised, though boat trips are arranged.

General Information: Nacionalni Park Skadarsko Jezero, Jerevanska 30, 81000 Titograd (tel: (081) 34-761 and 34-621).

◆◆
SKOPJE
Macedonia

Macedonia's capital hit the headlines in 1963, when it was at the epicentre of a powerful earthquake. Half the town was destroyed and 1,000 people died. It has been rebuilt and restored since; only the old railway station façade, with its clock stopped at 05.16 hours, the time of the first tremor, remains as a reminder of the disaster.
There has been settlement here for some 6,000 years, but the city was probably founded by the Roman emperor Justinian. During its history, it shared the fate of many Yugoslavian towns, coming under the rule of successive occupiers. Many of the surviving old buildings date from the longest such rule – that of the Ottoman Turks.

Sightseeing

The rebuilt new town is linked to the old town by the pedestrian **Kameni Most,** a 15th-century stone bridge over the River Vardar, which miraculously survived the earthquake. Sights in the old town include the **Čaršija,** or bazaar quarter, now largely a tourist trap with few true craftsmen at work. More interesting is the **Pit Pazar,** a weekend open market where people from the surrounding country come to sell their products. Of several mosques, the best is the 15th-century **Mustafa Pasha;** to the west of it, on a hill, is the impressive **Skopsko Kale,** the Turkish fortress. The church of **Sveti Spas** (the Saviour) is notable for a magnificent carved wooden iconostasis.
Prirodnjački Muzej Makedonije (Museum of Macedonia), Bulevar Ilinden 86, was built to house a number of collections from museums destroyed in the earthquake (Archaeological, Ethnographic and Historical).
Open: daily (except Monday) 08.00–19.00 hrs (June to August), until 18.00 hrs (April, May and September); until 17.00 hrs (March and October); and until 16.00 hrs (November to February).
Outside and above the town is the village of Nerezi with a wonderful view over Skopje. The monastery church of **Sveti Panteleimon** here has 12th-century frescos which are some of the finest in the country.

Accommodation

There are two A and four B category hotels listed. The A category **Grand Hotel Skopje** (tel: (091) 239-311) has 256 beds. Smaller are the B category **Bellevue** (tel: (091) 223-474) with 80 beds and **Bristol** (tel: (091) 239-821) with 74 beds. Private rooms and other cheap accommodation are hard to come by.

PEACE AND QUIET

Yugoslavia's Wildlife and Countryside

by Paul Sterry

Yugoslavia boasts one of the most varied landscapes in the whole of Europe: from a complex and stunning coastline the land rises through forested hills to bare mountain peaks above the tree line. Geological forces and erosion have enhanced Yugoslavia's scenic beauty, forming steep valleys and gorges and, where limestone predominates, extensive cave systems.
With this variety in habitat, it is not surprising that the natural history interest of Yugoslavia is rich. Visitors can expect to find almost all the elements of Mediterranean wildlife present

Lake Bohinj, in Slovenia

on the coast with truly alpine species found on the mountain tops.
Compared to many countries around the Mediterranean, the Yugoslavian countryside is relatively unspoilt. The coastline is as attractive as it is dramatic and the wooded hills and mountains are also comparatively untouched, partly due to their inaccessibility and partly because of the importance of forestry. Unfortunately, the same cannot be said about the wetlands and rivers, many of which have been drained or altered irreparably. Despite this, however, lakes and marshes still survive where, at the right times of year, thousands of waterbirds congregate.

PEACE AND QUIET

Limestone cliffs, Montenegro

Coast and Sea

On the Dalmatian coast of Yugoslavia, bathed by the warm waters of the Adriatic, the beauty of the rugged shores is enhanced by hundreds of small offshore islands and outcrops which together provide a stunning setting for the coastal plants and animals.

Birdlife along the coast is not particularly varied, especially when compared to the wealth of species found around Yugoslavia's wetlands. However, herring gulls of the yellow-legged Mediterranean race are often seen and sometimes congregate around harbours and ports. Alongside them, a careful search may reveal black-headed gulls and perhaps even Mediterranean or slender-billed gulls as well.

Offshore, shags swim low in the water while Manx shearwaters, and possibly even Cory's shearwaters, skim by on outstretched wings. Yugoslavia is on the migration route for many birds heading to other parts of Europe. During spring and autumn, coastal scrub should be searched in the early morning for warblers and other songbirds while the shoreline may harbour resting waders, egrets or herons.

Although the small tidal range of the Adriatic means that very little shoreline is exposed at low tide, it also means that the beaches are often more stable for plant colonisation. Rocky areas support sea lavender while beaches of loose sand and gravel soon harbour cottonweed, purple spurge, rock samphire, sea bindweed and sea squill.

Coastal scrub and grassland can be 'alive' with insects in spring, including crickets, grasshoppers and butterflies such as bath white, clouded yellow, painted lady and swallowtail. Hermann's tortoises plod slowly through the vegetation and lay their eggs where the soil is loose enough, while Dalmatian wall lizards scurry at great speed to escape from danger.

Lizards have good reason to be alert since the Dalmatian coast is frequented by a variety of snakes, most notably the Balkan whip snake and the Montpelier snake, which prey upon them. The best time to observe and photograph both snakes and lizards is early in the morning and early in the year since they become very active in the heat of the sun. Those not inclined to watch snakes need have no fear

PEACE AND QUIET

because they normally disappear at the first signs of people and are only seen well with careful and quiet searching.

Maquis and Garrigue

One of the major attractions of Yugoslavia to the foreign visitor is the Mediterranean climate of its Dalmatian coast which produces hot, dry summers and mild, damp winters. Being the most equable region of the country it has been most affected by man and, in common with the rest of the Mediterranean region, considerable areas of natural woodland have been cleared. In Yugoslavia, man's impact has been less dramatic than in some other countries and, as a result, almost all the typical Mediterranean plants and animals can be found among fine examples of the region's most characteristic habitats – the open, stony *garrigue* and the more lush, bushy *maquis*. For most of the year, much of this open country appears dry and scorched but in late winter and early spring, a wealth of flowers appears. Where Aleppo pine or holm oak provide shade, an understorey of strawberry tree, carob, and tree heathers develops, while cistuses and juniper often thrive in more open situations. Often growing on the most unpromising soils a good selection of orchids can be found in spring with names often as extraordinary as the appearance of their flowers: naked man orchids, tongue orchids, bumblebee and yellow bee orchids are among these. The display of flowers we enjoy is, of course, provided to attract pollinating insects. Metallic chafer beetles, hoverflies, hummingbird hawk moths and colourful butterflies such as green hairstreaks, Cleopatras, tree graylings and southern festoons may all be seen visiting from time to time. Crickets and bush crickets feed at ground level and are eaten by Turkish geckos, green lizards and wall lizards, which in turn may fall victim to leopard snakes, cat snakes or nose-horned vipers. The birds of the *maquis* and *garrigue* are varied and interesting, but patience and persistence is often required to get good views. Sardinian, sub-alpine, Orphean and olivaceous warblers skulk among the bushes while black-eared wheatears often perch on exposed rocks and scold intruders into their territory. Black-headed buntings use overhead wires and dead branches as song perches and are sometimes joined by bee-eaters. These elegant, burrow-nesting birds are perhaps the most strikingly colourful birds to be found in Yugoslavia.

A southern festoon

PEACE AND QUIET

Lakes and Marshes
Yugoslavia still possesses some fine lakes and areas of marsh despite the constant threat of reclamation and development. These areas are full of colourful marshland flowers in spring and support thriving communities of fish, amphibians and other aquatic creatures. In turn, this ensures the survival of rich and varied communities of nesting and wintering water birds as well as providing food for thousands of migrants.

On the border with Albania in southern Yugoslavia, lie **Ohridsko Ezero** Lake Ohrid and **Prespansko Ezero** (Lake Prespa). Although the shorelines are comparatively rocky and barren, in places gently shelving beaches may harbour grey herons, ruff and wood sandpipers during migration time. The lakes are well known for their fish populations, several species of which are endemic, and these are food for fish-eating birds such as cormorants, several species of wintering ducks and white and Dalmatian pelicans.

To the south of Titograd, **Skadarsko Jezero** (Lake Skadar or Scutari) also straddles the border between Yugoslavia and Albania. Although a boat is really needed, good views across reedbeds and marshes can be had to the south of the causeway. European pond terrapins scuttle through the water and, in the spring, a chorus of marsh frogs, common frogs and tree frogs have to compete with Cetti's and great reed warblers. Harriers quarter the reedbeds while squacco, night, purple and grey herons stalk the shallow margins. The lake is, perhaps, best known for its colony of Dalmatian pelicans and distant birds can sometimes be seen on the water or in flight.

Hutovo Blato Natural Reserve near Metkovic is a protected area of marshes, reedbeds and pools which can be viewed from the road that runs along its edge. Spring sees the emergence of colourful swallowtail butterflies and marsh orchids as well as the arrival of wetland birds like great reed warblers, marsh harriers, pygmy cormorants, little egrets, little bitterns, purple herons and night herons.

Triglav National Park
Nacionalni Park Triglav lies in the extreme northwest of Yugoslavia close to the border with Italy. The park has an interesting range of habitats, from Mediterranean vegetation

Scenery at Lake Ohrid

PEACE AND QUIET

on the lower slopes to truly alpine communities above the tree line. Glaciation and weathering have eroded the limestone of the Julian Alps and produced some of the most dramatic scenery in the whole of the country: seven glacial lakes and a magnificent waterfall form a centrepiece to the park and are overlooked by jagged peaks with the Triglav Mountain itself reaching 9,393 feet (2,863m).

The lower slopes have extensive woodlands of beech under which grow a variety of orchids and woodland fungi while at higher elevations larch and pine predominate. Wildcats and martens occur but are shy and difficult to see. Woodland birds are easier to find. Perhaps most noticeable are the woodpeckers, of which several species occur. Great-spotted and middle-spotted woodpeckers are comparatively widespread and there is a chance of seeing more unusual species such as black or white-backed woodpeckers. Towards the tree line, rocky outcrops and scree slopes support only stunted trees and clumps of alpenrose but may harbour rock buntings, rock thrushes, rock partridges and water pipits. Ptarmigan and mountain hares can be found at higher elevations but it takes a keen eye to spot them. Chamois are easier to see but difficult to approach. Their sure-footed confidence on broken terrain and above precipitous drops means they can go where few other creatures dare to venture. The alpine meadows in Triglav National Park are a wonderful sight in spring with a dazzling array of colourful flowers; globeflowers, orchids and spring gentians greet the eye in profusion. Later in the season, bush crickets and grasshoppers scurry through the vegetation while the flowers are visited by large and showy Apollo butterflies.

Plitvice Lakes National Park
Lying in the northwest of Yugoslavia, Plitvička Jezera (the Plitvice Lakes) are one of the country's most popular national parks. Despite the large number of people that visit the park, careful management and a fine network of trails and viewpoints ensure that the visitor's effect on the environment is minimised and the scenery remains stunning and unspoilt.

Within the boundaries of Plitvice lies a series of lakes which descend through the park, their waters an amazing range of blues and greens. Huge torrents cascade down from lake to lake and the dramatic waterfalls are made even more imposing by the build-up of travertine formations (chalky deposits). With the water as the centrepiece of the park, much of the surrounding land is covered in forests of beech and fir.

In marked contrast to the austere mantle of snow in the winter months, spring and summer are seasons full of colour. Woodland clearings and meadows abound with primroses, cowslips, spiked rampion, crocuses, bellflowers,

PEACE AND QUIET

hellebores and cyclamens.
These in turn attract a range of
colourful beetles, flies and
butterflies such as green
hairstreak, large tortoiseshell
and Camberwell beauty.
Although less numerous,
martagon lily and orchids such
as bird's nest orchid, red
helleborine, lady orchid and
lady's slipper orchid are well
worth searching for.

The forests of Nacionalni Park
Plitvička Jezera harbour a wide
range of birds which are best
observed in spring and early
summer when they are singing
or displaying. Several species of
woodpecker can be heard
'drumming', while flycatchers
and warblers are vigorous
songsters. On sunny days, honey
buzzards or golden eagles may
soar overhead.

The woodlands also harbour shy
mammals which survive due to
the lack of persecution.

Plitvice Lakes National Park

Wildcats, foxes, roe deer and
wild boar are all present and
best searched for away from
populated areas, as are the
park's brown bears. Because
they are not hunted here, a
healthy bear population exists in
Plitvice and individuals roam
widely in search of fruit, berries
and carrion.

Mljet National Park

In stark contrast to the dramatic,
mountainous landscape of
inland Yugoslavia, the Adriatic
coast and its offshore islands
have a typically Mediterranean
'feel' to them. Although most of
the coastline is beautiful and
relatively unspoilt, the limestone
island of Mljet, off the coast
north of Dubrovnik, is
particularly outstanding. Bathed
by azure waters, it is a wonderful
spot to spend a relaxing holiday

PEACE AND QUIET

while observing a wide range of plants and animals.
Although parts of the island have felt the destructive influence of man, the boundaries of Nacionalni Park Mljet protect some fine areas of woodland, *maquis* and coastline in the northwest corner of the island. Here are almost all the classic elements of Mediterranean flora and fauna. In common with many areas of the Mediterranean, woodland thrives on Mljet where it is left untouched. Holm oak, stone pine and Aleppo pine are the dominant trees and a rich, shrub community, known as *maquis*, develops underneath. This comprises strawberry tree, juniper, myrtle, heathers, cistuses and a range of orchids. The colourful flowers are visited by metallic-looking chafer beetles and butterflies such as green hairstreak and southern white admiral. Day-flying moths such as hummingbird hawk moths and silver-striped hawk moths, whose rapid wing beats turn their movement into a blur, also feed here, using their long tongues to feed on the wing.
The shrubs of the *maquis* are full of bird song in spring with the birds often being easier to hear than to see. Early morning is generally the most productive time of day and olivaceous, Sardinian, Orphean and sub-alpine warblers should be found by persistent searching. Because the island lies on the coast, it also receives large numbers of migrant birds on passage and several species of warblers and flycatchers, as well as black-eared wheatears

and black-headed buntings may turn up from March to May. Parties of colourful bee-eaters pass through both in spring and autumn and late summer sees the appearance of rollers and birds of prey making their way south along the coast.

Lovćen National Park

Nacionalni Park Lovćen lies to the south of Dubrovnik in southwest Yugoslavia at the southeast end of the Dinaric Alps. Despite its proximity to the coast, the park rises to nearly 5,750 feet (1,750m) above sea-level and on clear days, magnificent views can be had along the Adriatic coast and of the Gulf of Kotor (Boka Kotorska) in particular.
At first glance, the higher elevations of the park are rather bleak and forbidding, especially on an overcast day; this is one of the wettest parts of Yugoslavia and centuries of weathering and erosion by wind and rain have produced the limestone plateau landscape known as *karst*.
The porous nature of the soil means that water drains away quickly but in broad depressions (known as *polja*) and small, damp hollows (known as *dolinas*) a comparatively rich variety of flowers may be found including irises, orchids, sage and thyme. The lower slopes of Lovćen are still covered in patches of woodland comprising hop-hornbeam and white oak, sometimes with an interesting understorey of flowering plants. In spring the trees may hold migrant collared and red-breasted flycatchers and warblers, as well as resident

PEACE AND QUIET

bird species. Wolves, beech martens and wildcats also occur but are much more difficult to see.

Open scree slopes often harbour a surprising variety of flowers in spring and are also home to rock partridges. Ravens, recognised by their all-black plumage and wedge-shaped tail, and griffon vultures soar overhead, on the lookout for carrion on the ground below. The skies above Lovćen are also frequented by more active predators such as golden eagles, peregrines and short-toed eagles, with the latter specialising in catching snakes in the open terrain.

Mavrovo National Park

Lying in the south of the country on the Albanian border, Nacionalni Park Mavrovo is Yugoslavia's largest national park and one of its most attractive. Forests of beech and spruce give way to colourful alpine meadows above the tree line and finally to mountains which, in the west of the park, exceed 8,800 feet (2,700m). The variety in the scenery is reflected in the wealth of plants and animals found here, which include some of Europe's most exciting mammals and birds. Despite persecution in the past, which continues to a lesser extent to this day, brown bears survive in good numbers, throughout the country, and Mavrovo is one of their strongholds. Lynx and wolves also live here, and the eerie calls of the latter species can sometimes be heard in late summer.

Clearings on the lower wooded slopes of Mavrovo have a carpet of interesting flowers including butterfly orchids, bellflowers and cranesbills and are the haunt of butterflies such as Camberwell beauty and southern white admiral. Coal tits, great tits, chiffchaffs and goldcrests forage for insects among the foliage while buzzards and sparrowhawks soar overhead.

Alpine meadows and scree slopes hold a variety of flowers such as spring gentians, stonecrops, cowslips, violets and milk-vetches and are home to alpine choughs, alpine accentors, snow finches and rock buntings. Alpine swifts and peregrines haunt the skies, and golden eagles and griffon vultures are sometimes seen. Although the range of birds of prey in Mavrovo National Park is good, **Babuna Kanjon** (Babuna Gorge), which lies to the east of the park to the south of Skopje, generally provides greater variety and easier viewing. Griffon and Egyptian vultures are frequent and black vultures and lammergeiers are regularly recorded. Booted and golden eagles sometimes appear and migrating birds of prey, storks, pelicans and swallows and martins add to the interest.

Galičica and Pelister National Parks

These are the two southernmost national parks in Yugoslavia and both lie close to the Albanian and Greek borders; Nacionalni Park Galičica sits between Lakes Ohrid and Prespa while Nacionalni Park Pelister is

PEACE AND QUIET

situated a short distance to the east. With terrain that varies from the tranquil shores of the lakes through dense forest to alpine meadows and mountain tops over 6,000 feet (2,000m), the region as a whole has plenty to offer the visitor.

Although Galičica and Pelister are in close proximity to one another and both have mountainous upland regions, the extensive forests which cloak their lower slopes differ markedly. Pelister is characterised by woodlands of Macedonian pine with an understorey of bracken and bilberry, while in Galičica, Macedonian oak, beech and mixed deciduous woodlands predominate.

Depending on the altitude at which the woodland grows and the amount of light penetrating to the woodland floor, any of a variety of plants such as hellebores, crocuses, violets, mezereon, wood cranesbill, peach-leaved bellflower and coralroot bittercress may be found. Spring gentian, spring sandwort, rock-rose and sticky catchfly prefer more open situations, such as meadows and stony slopes where rock bunting, rock thrush and rock nuthatch may be found as well. Throughout the region, the lower wooded slopes provide nesting sites for red kites, buzzards and sparrowhawks. The extensive forests also harbour wolves and European brown bears, the latter being most frequently seen in Pelister. Here the bears are given a degree of protection and in this sparsely populated region their

Peach-leaved bellflower

numbers hold their own. Red deer, wild boar and wolves also occur and the secretive lynx may still be present, although you would be fortunate indeed to see one.

Sutjeska National Park
Nacionalni Park Sutjeska lies to the north of Dubrovnik and comprises forest, mountains, alpine meadows, lake and rivers. While the scenery is always dramatic and stunning, much of the land has been affected by man to a greater or lesser extent. This particularly applies to the woodland, but fortunately the Peručica reserve within the park's boundaries strictly protects a wonderful area of virgin forest from interference.

Woodland throughout the park

PEACE AND QUIET

is mainly a mixture of deciduous trees such as maple, oak and ash at lower altitudes while at higher elevations, beech and finally mountain pine predominate. Fly honeysuckle, elder, spurge laurel and birthwort form an understorey, flowers such as violets, purple coltsfoot and alpine snowbell preferring more open areas. Birds of prey such as buzzards and goshawks circle over forested slopes which echo with the loud calls of black woodpeckers. Capercaillies, brown bears and wolves are also retiring residents of the woodlands, while chamois prefer the higher, stony slopes along with rock nuthatches and rock thrushes.

Durmitor and Biogradska Gora National Parks

Durmitor is perhaps best known for Tara Kanjon (Tara Gorge) which, in places, is more than 3,200 feet (1,000m) deep. However, Nacionalni Park Durmitor also holds splendid *karst* landscapes together with forests, glacial lakes, alpine meadows and mountains.
The woodlands harbour small numbers of brown bears as well as woodland birds such as woodpeckers and capercaillie. Rock partridges prefer open terrain at higher altitudes, and rock faces, as well as gorges, are the haunt of such birds as crag martins, peregrines and wallcreepers. The latter prefer shady rock faces, with trickling water, to search for insects in the crevices.
In clearings and open stretches of woodland, the understorey includes flowers such as herb paris, Martagon lily and wood cranesbill, which are at their best in late spring. From May to July, the meadows are also colourful with bellflowers, bistort and black vanilla orchids at lower altitudes, and spring gentian, alpine snowbell, mountain avens and moss campion dazzling the eye at higher elevations.
Situated to the northeast of Titograd, Nacionalni Park Biogradska Gora comprises virgin forest and glacial lakes in the Bjelasica mountains.

Postojna Caves

Erosion by water of Yugoslavia's limestone rocks has produced some dramatic scenery, most noticeably the *karst* landscape and deep gorges. This same erosion occurs unseen as the water filters through the rock, with the result that huge underground networks of caves have developed. Although many of these have never been explored, Postojnska Jama (Postojna Caves) in the northwest of the country have amazing formations of stalagmites and stalactites (see also page 73). So ancient and extensive is the network of caves in Yugoslavia that a unique range of animals has evolved to suit a lifetime in permanent darkness. Many species undoubtedly remain undiscovered, but cave-dwelling species of moth, spider, harvestman and crustaceans are all known. Most unusual of all, however, is the olm, an axolotl-like amphibian which retains larval features such as external gills.

FOOD AND DRINK

Korčula market: vegetables are available in meat-eating Yugoslavia

FOOD AND DRINK

Eating

Dainty eaters tend to have a hard time in Yugoslavia, where food is generally served in large quantities with a distinct lack of finesse. Vegetarians are also at a disadvantage, as meat is very much the basis of most dishes. However, eating out is not expensive (except in some hotels, in tourist-trap restaurants and – strangely on the coast – in fish restaurants), and there are some interesting and tasty local dishes to be tried.

The different republics have their own regional styles of cooking, but some dishes can be regarded as national. *Pihtije* is jellied pork or duck; *pršut* (= Italian *prosciutto*) is smoked ham, usually served in wafer-thin slices as an appetiser; *cevapčići* (small rolls of charcoal-grilled minced meat with raw onion) and *ražnići* (pork or veal kebab) can often be bought from street stalls, as can *burek* (pasty filled with cheese, meat or apple). Other dishes (found throughout the Balkans) include *musaka* (aubergines with minced meat) and *sarma* (stuffed vine or cabbage leaves).

Northern Yugoslavia (Slovenia and north Croatia) reflects its Austrian-influenced past in its cuisine, with a preponderance of sausages, dumplings, *Strudel* and cream cakes. In Vojvodina, Hungarian flavours can be discerned, as in the rich meat or fish stew/soup, *paprikaš*. Turkish influence prevails in the dishes of Serbia, Bosnia-Hercegovina and Macedonia, with much use of aubergines, peppers and spices. A typical Serbian dish is *duveč*, mixed vegetables, meat and rice baked together in the oven; the Bosnian dish *Bosanski lonac* is a hotpot of meat and

FOOD AND DRINK/SHOPPING

vegetables (especially cabbage) cooked for many hours in a special earthenware pot. Along the Adriatic coast, the food shows Mediterranean influence, with the emphasis on fish and pasta.

You need a sweet tooth to enjoy Yugoslavian desserts, which include such ubiquitous Balkan favourites as *kadaif* (pastry with butter, sugar, nuts and raisins) and *baklava* (pastry with nuts and honey syrup). There is also *strukl* (balls made from nuts, plums and cheese) and *alva* (nuts crushed in honey).

The salty cream cheese called *kajmak* is Yugoslavia's best known cheese.

Drinking

Yugoslavia is a wine-producing country and there is no shortage of good (and cheap) table wines from a number of different regions.

Red wines include *Plavac* and *Dingač* from the Pelješac peninsula. *Teran* is another red, from Istria. Among white wines, the best known is the Slovenian *Risling* (much exported). The golden *Grk* from Korčula island is strong and should be drunk warily. Other whites are *Postup* (from Pelješac) and *Semion* ... but there are many more, both white and red.

The main spirit drink is *šlivovica* (plum brandy), which can be very nasty when it is cheap. Other liqueurs include *travarica* (with herbs), *vinjak* (a kind of cognac) and *maraskino* (sweet cherry liqueur).

Beer *(pivo)* is of a light lager-type. Coffee is usually served in the Turkish style – thick and very sweet (unless you ask for it with little or no sugar). Tea is generally undistinguished, except in the more oriental towns, where it comes strong, sweet and without milk, served in a small glass.

SHOPPING

Shopping in Yugoslavia often means very good value for visitors.

This applies particularly to products of natural materials like wool, cotton (particularly embroidery and lace), leather; also glass and crystal. They are of good quality, although they may lack the final touch of fashionable design.

There are regional variations of price and value. The better shops for general commodities, if not specialist souvenirs, are in the bigger towns, but prices here will be higher. And the more tourist-conscious places are more expensive. In the south for instance, a smart and serviceable large leatherette

Haggling is an accepted practice

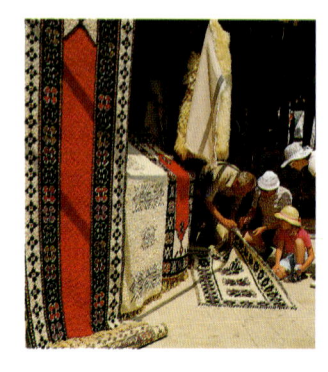

SHOPPING/ACCOMMODATION

suitcase could be bought for half the price of a smaller and gaudier hold-all in Pula on the Adriatic coast.

As against state chain-stores, where smiling attention is, sadly, rare, private shops and boutiques can offer more for the money – and they might accept foreign currency, provided it is cash (indeed some shops give 10 per cent discount for payment in foreign currency). The shopkeeper might even bargain with the polite haggler. The many open air markets can be a source of good buys, as well as being photogenic. 'Tourist traps' are infrequent, and mainly on the Adriatic coast.

Imported goods from surrounding east European countries, plus fur coats from Greece, Italian shoes and Chinese feather-down winter jackets, can be bought at much lower prices than in their countries of origin! Decent scissors, however, are hard to come by and visitors should be sure to bring their own.

Good hand-made articles are no longer very easy to find, but look out for filigree jewellery in Montenegro and the occasional piece of good lace or embroidery. Tourist resorts and larger towns have *Narodna Radinost* (folk craft) shops, selling hand-made articles.

ACCOMMODATION

Yugoslavia offers the full gamut of accommodation, from the luxury of the glamorous hotel-island of Sveti Stefan, through run-of-the-mill package

Hotel architecture is generally unobtrusive: Hotel Liburna, Korčula

hotels, to simple rooms in private houses.

Hotels come in five categories: L (de luxe), A, B, C and D. In C and D hotels you will have to share a bathroom, but bedrooms are not too expensive. There are **pensions** *(pansioni)* in three categories (I, II and III) – many privately run; establishments not covered by these standards are classified as inns.

Some tourist resorts, mainly on the coast, have **holiday villages** built near hotels with bungalows and pavilions (independent rooms grouped round a hotel). These are mainly for package tourists.

For stays of more than three days, hotels and pensions have fixed prices, including three meals a day.

Independent travellers by car may be interested in the **motels** that are springing up along main roads and at the approaches to towns. Petrol, sales and sometimes repair services are available here also.

Rooms let by private individuals usually offer the best bargain.

ACCOMMODATION/ENTERTAINMENT

To find out what is available and book a room, you can apply to the tourist office in the town in question, or – in larger resorts – travel agencies or even hotels can sometimes help. You will pay a surcharge if you use an agent of any sort. Private rooms are graded and priced according to comfort. The deal can sometimes include meals. To book a **furnished apartment** or **villa** (these are mainly available along the Adriatic coast), apply to one of the Yugoslav travel agencies or the tourist office in the resort you are interested in.

All kinds of accommodation get booked up in the high season in the more popular places, so it is advisable to book in advance. A list of hotels, motels and pensions, with prices quoted in German DM or US $, can be obtained from branches of the Yugoslav National Tourist Office.

CULTURE, ENTERTAINMENT AND NIGHTLIFE

Yugoslavia has its share of arts festivals, offering classical concerts, opera, ballet and drama, often in spectacular settings. (See **Special Events** page 105 for specific venues and dates.)

Folklore is an important part of local culture – some of it still alive and genuine. Even the special folklore performances put on for visitors in the main resorts often have more merit than similar shows in other countries. The national dance is the *kolo*, a circle dance, each region having its own variation. It used to be danced as an act of defiance to the Turks, as well as to promote fertility, deter evil spirits, etc.

Folk dancers, in colourful Dalmatian costume, at Čilipi near Cavtat

ENTERTAINMENT/WEATHER AND WHEN TO GO

One of the most celebrated traditional events is the *Moreška* (Moorish dance) from the island of Korčula. Once an annual event, it now takes place every Thursday during the summer season. It is a kind of sword dance/drama, each dancer wielding two swords.

'Peasant weddings' are another attraction for visitors. These are mass weddings, the participants resplendent in local costume. They may be seen in, for example, Plitvice at the end of May, Ljubljana in late June and Bohinjska Bistrica in mid-July. Travellers off the beaten track may be lucky enough to witness spontaneous folk happenings. Certainly, national costume is still worn everyday in some regions – sometimes taking bizarre forms as in the hills of Kosovo, where some village women wear a flat board under their wide skirts, like a kind of bustle. In the villages of the far south a descendant of the old epic singers of Homeric tradition may still occasionally be heard, accompanied by the one-stringed lute called a *guslar*.

In coastal Dalmatia, a world away from rural Macedonia or Montenegro, the style of impromptu singing you might hear is *klapa*, songs performed in up to six parts.

There is no lack of nightlife in the larger resorts, with discos and night-clubs in many hotels (often shattering the peace of a balmy summer night with their music). Night-clubs as a rule stay open until 03.00 hours, cinemas until 23.00 hours and restaurants to midnight.

The larger towns have a lively café life – particularly the university town of Ljubljana. For local young people everywhere, the regular evening event is the *Korso*, the promenade during which groups of girls and youths eye each other (but rarely get together).

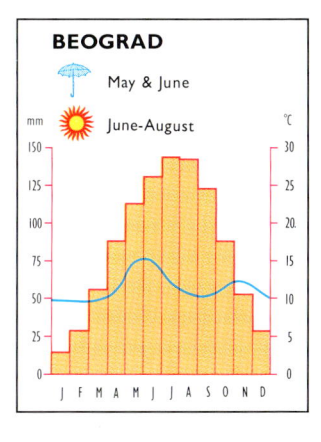

BEOGRAD

May & June
June-August

WEATHER AND WHEN TO GO

The climate varies widely. The north is continental; the mountains are alpine; the Adriatic coast is Mediterranean; and the central plain has a continental climate with cold winters and warm summers. Spring comes very early to the Adriatic coast. As early as March everything is in full bloom and the days are pleasant and warm. The coast is renowned for its 'insolation', with well over 2,500 hours of sunshine a year in many places. But strong winds, usually of short duration, can blow up quickly. The autumn is pleasant

WEATHER/HOW TO BE A LOCAL

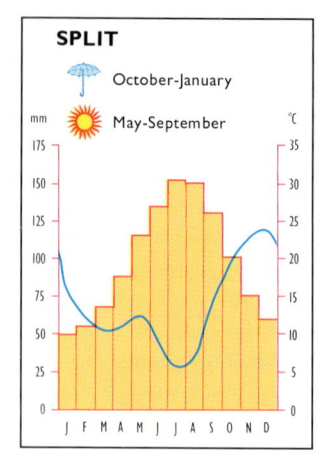

SPLIT

October–January
May–September

too and is usually warm and sunny. There is snow in the mountains from December until the end of March – and later in some high-altitude resorts – providing excellent conditions for winter sports.

The lowland interior of the country should be avoided in high summer, when the heat can be crippling. It is cooler in the hills, but travellers should expect rain at any time and come suitably shod and equipped with a waterproof. The popular areas become very crowded in summer. A low-season visit is not only pleasanter in avoiding the crowds and extreme heat, but also cheaper, as many hotels offer good discounts.

HOW TO BE A LOCAL

There is not space here for detailed advice on close integration, behavioural niceties, and customs in all parts of such a diversely populated country as Yugoslavia.

As guidance, it would be unwise to place much reliance on each region's stereotypical, exaggerated, or plain false picture of its own folk and (sometimes in joky insults) the people of other regions.

For instance: all Slovenians and Croatians are hard-working and businesslike (or Croatians somewhat dour and mean in the rustic north, while southerly Dalmatians are ardent lovers); Serbs are conservative and too big for their boots; Vojvodinars are earthy peasants; Kosovo Albanians are all fiercely feudal; Bosnians are large amiable comedians or buffoons; Montenegrins and Macedonians are proud, traditionalist fighters for honour – or play-actors with fancy moustaches.

Do's and Don't's

For the tourist, these brief attitudinal hints are offered by a Vojvodina-born Beograd University graduate, following some years as an expert guide travelling all over the country:

Expect slow motion to be the pace of living in Yugoslavia – then everything will come much easier.

Do not argue with officials, even if you are disturbed. They are probably not being unhelpful, but perhaps may not always understand your language – especially if spoken rapidly – as well as their use of it may suggest.

In the areas where Muslims live (central and south) do not (if male) pay attention to their women at all.

Do not wear 'immodest',

HOW TO BE A LOCAL/PERSONAL PRIORITIES

revealing attire if you visit a worshippers' mosque, church or monastery.

In religious buildings it is best to ask permission of any attendant before taking photographs; this is sometimes forbidden, as signs should indicate – for reasons of reverence, possible flash-light damage to delicate old frescos, or perhaps the need for the shop counter to sell colour transparencies and postcards. Except in hotels, restaurants, taxis and with porters, do not try to tip people for personal favours or advice; this could offend, as gratuity is not expected for a willing kindness. *Hvala* means 'thank you'; *Molim*, 'please' (in Serbo-Croat).

Do not expect smiles from assistants and officials in shops, banks, and some other offices. Their seriousness is their way of showing how hard they work. However, if they met you socially, in the street or a bar, they might well invite you into their homes for a polite chat and drink.

PERSONAL PRIORITIES

Females and Families

Women are unlikely to be seriously harassed, although on the Adriatic coast the Mediterranean male attitude of regarding foreign women as fair game may be encountered. A firm indication of disapproval is usually enough to discourage all but the most persistent pest.

In unsophisticated Muslim areas, women must be prepared to be regarded as second-class citizens, and should be careful not to give offence by dressing immodestly. Anywhere off the tourist trail, a woman sitting alone in a café or bar may have to suffer surprised stares. Sanitary towels are available from pharmacies and department stores. Tampons are not easy to come by; it is wise to carry a supply.

For families with small children, it is similarly advisable to take from home supplies of nappies, babyfoods, toiletries, sun lotion, first aid requisites, etc, as such items are not always easily obtainable. Even soap becomes a rarity off the beaten track – so is a plug in your washbasin or bath, so take a universal one.

Smoking

Smoking is prohibited on public transport, in cinemas, theatres, public offices and waiting rooms.

Naturism

The Yugoslav Adriatic coast and islands, with peaceful and untouched bays and beaches, offer ideal conditions for naturists. Naturist beaches have existed for decades already in certain areas (such as the island of Rab), and their number has been constantly growing. There are now a total of 30 naturist beaches with amenities, and many other beaches without special facilities where it is possible to sunbathe nude. The larger naturist beaches are well-equipped; they have full sanitary facilities, restaurants, shops, sports grounds, etc. Favourite naturist beaches are located on the islands of Cres, Krk, Lošinj, Kornati Archipelago, Korčula, Hvar and Brač, Rovinj, Cavtat, the Rivieras of Makarska

PERSONAL PRIORITIES/CHILDREN/TIGHT BUDGET

and Dubrovnik and at Ulcinj with its long sandy beaches. In addition, the great number of remote coves and uninhabited islands, accessible only by boat, makes it easy for anyone who enjoys nude bathing to find complete privacy.

CHILDREN

The Disneyland culture has not yet come to Yugoslavia, so the main attractions for children are the beaches and sea of the Adriatic coast. Not every resort caters particularly well for families with children, but some do offer special facilities. One mile from Budva, on the Montenegrin coast, is **Slovenska Plaža,** a self-contained holiday village, very safe for children. There is a long, coarse sand and pebble beach, children's play areas and provision of cots and high chairs for babies and toddlers. **Lopar,** on the island of Rab, has a particularly safe, sandy beach with play facilities for children; **Ulcinj,** in the deep south near the Albanian border, also has an excellent beach for youngsters, and hotels that cater well for families.

For a day off the beach, boat excursions to or between islands make a pleasant distraction. If staying in the north, older children would probably enjoy trips to the spectacular **caves of Postojna** and **Škocjan** (see pages 73 and 74). A visit to Lipica and its famous stud farm (see page 70) might also go down well.

The Yugoslavs like children and have a relaxed attitude towards them, so there should be no problem taking children into restaurants or cafés.

TIGHT BUDGET

Nobody need spend a fortune in Yugoslavia, but there are ways of making a stay even cheaper. In restaurants, order the simpler meals, Kebabs and sausages are cheap, and still have considerably more real meat content than in some Western countries. Fried cheese-and-bread is filling, and even cheaper.

For a snack, a bakery is often the best bet. Items can range from Cornish-pasty-type confections *(burek)* to honeyed doughnuts and *baklava*. Street stalls are also a good source of cheap, filling food.

Do not buy food on the beach or in places with large concentrations of tourists, though local food products like cheese and wine cost little.

For somewhere reasonable to stay, rooms in private houses can be recommended (see **Accommodation** page 99). However, they are quickly snapped up, so it is advisable to start looking as soon as you arrive where you want to stay. In high season, university towns offer rooms in student halls of residence, which are excellent value.

Many hotel and private rented rooms are let at a discount in low season, so you will certainly save money (and avoid the crowds) if you can travel then. For camping, see **Directory** page 112. Travel is cheap if you use buses – especially away from the coast. Hitch-hiking is

TIGHT BUDGET/SPECIAL EVENTS

not advisable, as Yugoslav drivers are suspicious of foreigners (who are expected to have money) trying to travel free. For special youth travel facilities, see **Directory** page 121.

SPECIAL EVENTS

The Yugoslav National Tourist Office publishes an annual calendar of events with details of festivals, fairs and sporting events throughout the country. A selection of annual events is given below.

April
Zagreb: International Spring Fair and tourism exhibition (Ferial).

May
Novi Sad: Yugoslav Theatre Festival
Plitvice: 'Plitvice Wedding' – folklore event
Skopje: opera evenings, featuring Yugoslav and international artists
Split: international Flower Show
Beograd: 'Skardalija Evenings' – exhibitions, music, theatre and folklore performances in Beograd's 'Bohemian' quarter, from May to December
Korčula: *Moreška* sword dance – performed on Thursdays, May to September

June/July
Ljubljana: Jazz Festival; *Ohcet v Ljubljani* (mass wedding folklore event)
Ohrid: Festival of Old Town Songs (Macedonian folk music); Balkan Festival of Original Folk Dances
Opatija: Summer Festival – open air music, drama, ballet, film

National Folk Ensemble at Hvar

and folklore performances, June to September
Split: 'Melodies of the Adriatic', light music festival
Zagreb: 'Summer in Zagreb' – open air peformances of plays, concerts, etc, June to August

July
Bled: Summer Festival
Bohinjska Bistrica: mass wedding – folklore event
Mostar: traditional diving competition from the Old Bridge (27 July)
Subotica: *Dužijanka* – traditional harvest festival
Zagreb: International Review of Original Folklore, held in the city's streets and squares.

July/August
Ohrid: Summer Festival – music, drama, ballet, folklore events
Pula: Festival of Yugoslav Films, held in the Roman amphitheatre
Rijeka: Cultural Summer Festival
Sarajevo: Summer Festival – music, drama and art exhibitions in the old town
Split: Summer Festival – music, drama, ballet and folklore events

SPECIAL EVENTS/SPORT

August
Bled: peasant wedding – folklore event

September
Beograd: Beograd International Theatre Festival (BITEF) – important avant-garde theatre event

October
Beograd: Beograd Music Festival (BEMUS) – concerts, ballet and opera featuring international artists
Zagreb: International Jazz Fair

October/November
Beograd: Salon of Fine and Applied Arts; Jazz Festival

SPORT

Fishing
Freshwater and sea fishing in Yugoslavia is rich in possibilities and variety, but it does not seem to be widely organised for visitors. You need a permit to fish in the country's rivers and lakes, issued by angling clubs, municipal authorities or sometimes by hotels. A fishing tax is also payable.

The 1,850 rivers of Yugoslavia give anglers a wide choice of catch – trout, grayling and charr in the mountain regions, and carp, pike, perch, perch-pike and sheatfish (a large freshwater catfish) in lowland rivers.

The Yugoslav Adriatic is very clear (rarely algae), especially in the south. Fishing in and under it, especially around the islands, has many attractions. There are said to be 365 kinds of Adriatic fish – mullet, mackerel, seabream, seabass, common dentex, eel, squid and octopus being among the most common. An international underwater fishing competition is held annually in December on the island of Lošinj.

Bohinjsko Jezero and Krnsko Jezero, beautiful mountain-surrounded lakes, contain a very highly esteemed lake trout known as *jezerska zlatovčica*. Additional information can be obtained from: Zavod za Ribištvo (Institute for Fishing), Župančičeva, 61000 Ljubljana (tel: (061) 214-934).

Fishing is not allowed in marine nature reserves, ports, beaches and zones restricted by municipal authorities, and information about this should be obtained locally. Where fishing is allowed, the daily catch is limited to 11lbs (5kg).

Permits are issued by municipal authorities, or you can apply for membership of one of the Yugoslav sea fishing, underwater fishing or diving societies. Line fishing from the sea shore does not require a permit. The Yugoslav National Tourist Office can provide addresses of regional sport fishing federations.

Diving
Diving with apparatus and underwater cine filming is permitted except in some restricted zones, ports, waterways, for 330 yards (300m) around warships, or on the coast where there are military installations. Diving gear may not be used for fishing under water.

Supplies of oxygen for diving apparatus can be obtained in all main resorts. Local port

SPORT

authority offices may have various information.

Hunting

What the Yugoslavs call hunting is usually shooting. There is careful conservation of rare species, but mountains, forests and plains along the rivers, especially the Danube and Sava, offer plenty of scope for what is allowed.

Game animals include red, fallow and roe deer, bear (now rare in the rest of Europe), chamois, moufflon, and wild boar; and game birds include pheasant, grouse, partridge, wild duck and geese, and many others.

Small game and marsh bird 'hunting' reserves can be found on Skadarsko Jezero (Skadar Lake), the wilderness of Hutovo Blato near Mostar, or Kopački Rit nature reserve near the Hungarian border in the north. For details on hunting grounds for big game, contact Lovoturs, Petrovaradinska tvrdava, 21000 Novi Sad, Yugoslavia (tel: (021) 616-242 and 622-172). Hunting grounds are reached by car or by horse-drawn carts; those in high mountains on horseback. Accommodation is in small hunting lodges or hotels, and experienced guides and hunting wardens are available. Some Yugoslav and foreign tourist agencies can arrange hunting trips and, for another kind of shooting, photo safaris to some national parks.

Sailing

More than 1,250 miles (2,000km) of Adriatic coastline, and a diversity of coves, bays, inlets and channels between hundreds of islands, offer ideal conditions for sailing from Yugoslav harbours, though strong winds, usually of short duration, can blow up unexpectedly. In the last 15 years numerous modern and well furnished marinas have been built along the coast. Along the coast, rivers or numerous lakes there are often excellent facilities for rafting,

Windsurfers must be wary of sudden winds off the Adriatic coast

SPORT

canoeing, water-skiing, diving, windsurfing, etc.
On entering the coastal waters of Yugoslavia, a yacht – or other vessel – should sail for the nearest port open to international traffic. Its captain should apply to the port authorities for a sailing permit, valid for a year and allowing unlimited sailing in Yugoslav waters. Permits allow sailing and docking along the whole Adriatic coast, including the islands, excluding certain areas which indicate that sailing is not permitted.
A canoe or similar vessel, not longer than 10 feet (3m), and which has no motor, brought overland, does not require a permit.
A yacht, or other vessel, should have valid sailing documents issued by the relevant authorities, and members of the crew should possess documents issued in their home countries certifying that they are capable of sailing the yacht.
In case of shipwreck or bad weather, a yacht can dock in any harbour.
Supplies are available in most of the ports. In larger ones, from Umag to Bar, there are special installations for refuelling yachts.
Minor repairs are possible in many places along the coast and on the islands. Fuller repair services are based only in ports and special marinas for yachts.
Owners of yachts may leave their vessels in Yugoslavia over the winter or longer, either in well-sheltered coves, or in closed winter sheds, found at main resorts.
Hire of small yachts, or larger boats, fit for sailing or cruising, is possible in many Yugoslav ports.

Other Sports
Soccer is undoubtedly the most popular sport in Yugoslavia. There are countless football teams in numerous divisions, often with a game going on wherever there is space.
The larger cities have famous teams and impressive modern stadia.
For players of both sexes, **basketball** is a virtually unrivalled attraction, and tourist facilities may reflect this.
In **tennis,** Yugoslavia has produced notable international performers, and courts with various surfaces (not often grass) are available in public parks as well as innumerable holiday hotel complexes.
Skiing is a popular pastime with weekend sports-persons at the counry's various burgeoning ski resorts, and an increasing number of winter sports visitors are coming to enjoy the facilities in the mountains. For more information see under individual resorts.
Handball and **water-polo** are among runners-up as national preoccupations.
Golf is not yet much followed, but there are now two estimable courses – above Lake Bled and at Lipica, in Slovenia.
Horse riding is negotiable at some resorts – and especially Lipica.
Walking can be enjoyed in greater varieties of terrain and scenery than in almost any other European country.

DIRECTORY

Arriving	Entertainment	Post Office
Bathing	Information	Public Transport
Camping	Health	Senior Citizens
Crime	Holidays	Student and Youth
Customs	Media	Travel
Driving	Money Matters	Telephones
Electricity	Opening Times	Time
Embassies and	Personal Safety	Tipping
Consulates	Pharmacies	Toilets
Emergency	Photography	Tourist Offices
Telephone	Places of Worship	Travel Agencies
Numbers	Police	

Arriving

Hydrofoils ply in Yugoslav waters

Entry Formalities

Tourist Pass. Nationals of countries with which Yugoslavia has diplomatic or consular relations, coming to Yugoslavia as tourists, may spend up to 30 days in the country with a Tourist Pass. This is issued at frontier crossings (free to EC nationals, otherwise a nominal charge) on the production of a valid passport or identity card.

Passports and Visas. Non-tourists and those wishing to stay longer than 30 days must have a valid passport. A stay beyond 90 days requires permission from the local Yugoslavian authorities. Visas are required by all except nationals of EC countries (other than Greece) for stays of up to 90 days. Visas are issued by Yugoslav diplomatic or consular missions, on the day to personal callers, and free of charge to nationals of the US, Canada or Australia.

Travel to Yugoslavia

Yugoslavia has more than 115 international border crossings, 70 auxiliary checkpoints and five crossings for mountaineers.

By Air. JAT (Jugoslovenski Aerotransport) is the Yugoslav

DIRECTORY

national airline. Head office: Birčaninova 1/3, 11000 Beograd, tel: (011) 131-392 (international and domestic flights – booking) and (011) 138-416 (intercontinental flights – booking). JAT has over 50 representatives abroad.
Through its regular international lines, JAT links Beograd, Ljubljana, Zagreb and other international airports in Yugoslavia with cities in Europe, North America, North Africa, Australia and the Near East, including London, Birmingham, Manchester and Glasgow in the UK, plus New York, Montreal, Toronto, Sydney and Melbourne. From London to Beograd the approximate flight time is 2 hours and 30 minutes, and to Zagreb, 2 hours and 5 minutes. From New York to Zagreb takes around 10 hours and 30 minutes. Most scheduled international services arrive at Beograd, Dubrovnik, Ljubljana, Split or Zagreb airports:

Beograd Airport is at Surčin, 12 miles (20km) west of the city. Coaches run every 20-30 minutes for the 30-minute journey to the city. Return journey is from the JAT Terminal, Bulevar Revolucije 17a. Taxis are also available (20 minutes to the city).
Dubrovnik Airport is at Čilipi, 13 miles (22km) southeast of the city. JAT runs a regular coach service to town, or there is the public bus, journey time 30 minutes. Taxis take 20 minutes.
Ljubljana Airport is at Brnik, 21 miles (35km) from the town, 30 minutes by coach.
Split Airport is 15½ miles (25km) from the town which can be reached by JAT's regular bus services; taxis also available.
Zagreb Airport is at Pleso, 10 miles (17km) southwest of the city. JAT runs a coach every 30 minutes. A public bus runs every 15 minutes for the 20-minute journey to the city. Taxis are also available (travel time 15 minutes).
In addition many charter flights arrive at Pula and Rijeka airports. Other airports include Maribor, Osijek, Portorož, Sarajevo, Skopje, Titograd, Tivat and Zadar.
All Yugoslav airports along the coast and in the interior of the country are linked by JAT's domestic flights which have regular connections with international lines. (See also **Public Transport**.)
Adria Airways, based in Ljubljana, also operates a limited international network (for address see **Public Transport** page 119).
Airport Departure Tax. For passengers leaving from a Yugoslavian airport there is a departure tax to pay. The amount depends on which airport you leave from. Transit passengers and children under two are exempt from payment. If in any doubt, check at the airport upon arrival.

By Rail. Yugoslavia is linked up with all European countries by rail. Express and fast trains have through-carriages on lines to almost all the major European cities. These trains have couchettes, sleeping cars, buffet and dining cars.
Passenger cars can be transported by train to

DIRECTORY

Arriving at Korčula

Yugoslavia. During the summer, car-sleeper trains operate a weekly service from s'Hertogenbosch (Holland) and Schaerbeeck (Brussels – Belgium) to Ljubljana. From Ljubljana there is an overnight motorail service to Beograd. In addition, there are car-sleeper services from Boulogne, Brussels, s'Hertogenbosch and Paris to Milan, from where you can continue your journey by rail or road. For detailed information, contact major railway stations or travel agencies.

By Bus. Direct bus services link Yugoslavia with many countries, including Austria, Bulgaria, Denmark, Germany, France, Greece, Hungary, Italy, Romania, Sweden, Switzerland and Turkey, as well as the UK. A number of companies operate high season, daily departures, from London, taking around 36 hours to Zagreb, and 40 hours plus to Beograd.

By Sea. Many cruise liners call at Dubrovnik, Split and Kotor, but for most people entering Yugoslavia by sea the usual route is via Italy or Greece. Ferry-boats link the Yugoslav Adriatic coast with various Italian and Greek ports. Contact **Jadrolinija** (Yugoslav Sea Traffic Company), Obala Jugoslovenske Mornarice 16, Rijeka, (tel:(051) 22-356 or (051) 214-483), for details of most services.
In summer, fast comfortable hydrofoils run from larger Yugoslavian ports to certain towns on the Italian coast. Yachtsmen sailing their own vessels into Yugoslav waters should register at the harbour master's office in the nearest port open to international traffic, where passport and customs formalities can be dealt with and a sailing permit obtained. Tourists who transport their vessels overland should obtain the permit at the port where they launch their vessels. The permit is valid for a year and allows sailing and docking along most of the Yugoslav coast. The owner or captain is obliged to report to the harbour master's office every time he leaves or re-enters Yugoslav coastal waters.

DIRECTORY

Bathing
The Adriatic is one of the most translucent seas of the world, and Yugoslavia has so far been largely successful in keeping away the algal blooms which have affected other parts of the Adriatic. The surface water temperature in summer averages around 25°C (77°F) all along the coast. There are many bays and coves which offer splendid isolation for swimming and sunbathing. The beaches are mainly shingle or pebble – with a few sandy exceptions, notably on some islands and, in the south, where there are extensive sands near Ulcinj. Rock bathing is ideal for those who enjoy snorkelling and scuba-diving. For information on naturist beaches see page 103.

Camping
There are over 300 camp sites in Yugoslavia, about half of them by the sea, some on islands. To preserve the natural unspoilt beauty of the countryside, camping is allowed only on organised sites, unless special permission is obtained from local authorities.

There is a charge for the use of camping sites, varying according to the standard. Many sites have electrical supply, full sanitary facilities, shops and areas for sporting activities. Food can be obtained on many sites and there are usually restaurants nearby. The hiring of camping equipment is possible at some sites. Accommodation in chalets or mountain-huts is also offered by some sites. A list of sites is available in Yugoslav National Tourist Offices.

Chemists (see Pharmacies)

Crime
Crime does not generally cause problems for visitors to Yugoslavia, but normal care of person and property should, of course, be exercised.

Customs Regulations
Besides normal personal luggage, visitors can take into the country technical goods (eg camera, transistor radio, cassette player, etc), sports and camping equipment for use during their stay. The following items may be imported without incurring customs duty by persons aged 16 or over: 200 cigarettes or 50 cigars or 250 grammes of tobacco, or a total of 250 grammes of all the above products; 0.75 litre of spirits; 1 litre of wine; 0.25 litre of eau-de-cologne; a small amount of perfume; and goods to a value of 1,000 dinars.

Currency. You can bring into, or take out of Yugoslavia, any amount of foreign currency, or its convertible equivalent. With local currency, however, you are limited, at time of writing, to 1,200 dinars per person on entering or leaving Yugoslavia.

Disabled Travellers
See **Senior Citizens**

Driving
Yugoslavia may be entered by car through frontier crossing points from Italy, Austria, Hungary, Romania, Bulgaria, Greece and Albania.
No customs documents are required for passenger cars and motorcycles. A car log-book, full national driving licence and a

DIRECTORY

'Green' or 'Blue' insurance card (which, if you do not have it, can be obtained from Yugoslav insurance companies at frontier crossings) is the only documentation required. If a driver has an accident, or for some other reason is unable to export his car on leaving Yugoslavia, it should be placed in the custody of the Customs authorities.

Roads
The Yugoslav road network has been greatly improved in recent years and the main tourist roads have a modern surface, although there are many minor roads which have only a macadam base, and some are downright rugged.
The highways in the northwest of the country are of an excellent standard. Highways link Ljubljana, Zagreb, Beograd, Novi Sad, Sarajevo and Titograd. The entire coast has a modern asphalt road, the 'Adriatic Highway' (E65), which ranks among the most attractive (and, in summer, crowded) tourist roads in Europe. This road, near the southernmost part of the coast at Petrovac, leads to the interior of the country and links up at Titova Mitrovica with the Ibar arterial road (Beograd–Skopje). The coast road, meanwhile, goes on to Albania. The main continental road, the E70, leads from the Italian and Austrian borders via Ljubljana, Zagreb, Beograd (after which it becomes the E75) on to Niš and the Bulgarian border and from Niš via Skopje, still on the E75, to the Greek border. Non-motorway sections should be driven with great care.
Motorways. Currently, around 560 miles (900km) of single and dual-carriageway motorway (*autoput* or *avtocesta*) are available, with further stretches under construction. Tolls are charged on most sections.

Mt Triglav: mountain roads are daunting but views are spectacular

DIRECTORY

Traffic regulations
Vehicles drive on the right-hand side of the road in Yugoslavia, or in the right-hand lane if there are several lanes. The other lanes are to be used for overtaking.

Vehicles must not exceed the prescribed speed limits. The speed limit in towns is 37mph (60kph), on motorways 75mph (120kph), on major roads 62mph (100kph) and on all other roads 50mph (80kph).

Foreign vehicles should clearly indicate the country of registration as well as their licence plates.

A vehicle should carry a red warning triangle which should be placed 55 yards (50m) behind the vehicle in the event of an accident.

Traffic signs in Yugoslavia correspond to the internationally recognised ones. The words *Jedan Smer*, on a blue and white arrow, indicate a one-way street in the direction of the arrow.

When towing, in the event of a breakdown, two triangles must be placed (side by side) at the back of the vehicle being towed.

The use of safety belts is obligatory in cars which are fitted with them. Children under 12 years of age must not ride in the front seat.

Trams have priority over all vehicles at all times.

It is forbidden to drive under the influence of alcohol.

It is compulsory for visiting motorists to carry a first-aid kit in their vehicles, and to equip themselves with a set of replacement bulbs.

For serious traffic violations, a

Scenic glory in the Julian Alps

driver with a foreign driver's licence will be forbidden to drive on Yugoslav territory for a specified time, which is marked on his driver's licence or international driver's licence.

Parking. This is often a problem in towns and main resorts. Restrictions exist in some of the larger towns in the 'blue' zone. Between 08.00 and 19.00 hrs, Monday to Saturday, parking meters are in use in some towns.

Fuel
Three grades are available: **Premium,** 86 octane; **Superior,** 98–100 octane; and leadfree petrol *(Bezolvni)*, 95 octane, as well as diesel fuel. There is no shortage of petrol stations in towns and along major roads, and many of these provide a 24-hour service. Credit cards are not accepted for the purchase of petrol.

Tourist petrol coupons, which may be purchased abroad and at Yugoslav frontier crossings with foreign currency, entitle

DIRECTORY

holders to a 5 per cent discount at any petrol station. Unused coupons can be refunded either at the Yugoslav border on leaving the country, or at offices of the Yugoslav Automobile Association (AMSJ).

Assistance
The *Auto-Moto Savez Jugoslavije* (AMSJ) and associations in the republics offer a full range of services and assistance to foreign motorists. The AMSJ has a large number of specialised vehicles for repairing and towing cars. Vehicles and mechanics are stationed at over 180 bases. In case of breakdown, a specialised vehicle can be called by telephone (see below) or with the assistance of a police patrol or a passing motorist.
The assistance-information bases are open from 08.00 to 20.00 hrs. During the tourist season in larger towns they provide a 24-hour service.
The introduction of a single number, 987, for the assistance-and-information service is being introduced and the AMSJ bases may be contacted at this number in many towns.
A list of lawyers who will advise foreign drivers is available from the AMSJ.

Car Rental
Cars are available from airports and main towns and resorts either through international car rental companies or travel agencies such as **Putnik, Kompas** and **Autotehna.** Sometimes there is the option of a chauffeur or a guide, but rental of a car alone can be quite expensive in Yugoslavia.

Electricity
The supply is 220 volts AC, 50 cycles, with sockets accepting circular, two-pin plugs. An adaptor is required for electrical appliances with other types of plug. A voltage transformer is required for appliances that run on a lower voltage at home and do not have a dual-voltage switch.

Embassies and Consulates

UK
Embassy: Generala Ždanova 46, **Beograd** (tel: (011) 645-055)
Consulate General: Ilica 12, **Zagreb** (tel: (041) 424-888)
Consulate: Titova Obala 10, **Split** (tel: (058) 41-464)
Consulate: Pile 1, **Dubrovnik** (tel: (050) 27-333)

US
Embassy: Kneza Miloša 50, **Beograd** (tel: (011) 645-655)
Consulate General: Braće Kavurića 2, **Zagreb** (tel: (041) 444-800)

Canada
Embassy: Kneza Miloša 75, **Beograd** (tel: (011) 644-666)

Australia
Embassy: Cjika Ljubina 13, **Beograd** (tel: (011) 624-655)

Emergency Telephone Numbers
In main towns:
Police 92
Fire 93
Ambulance 94
(Elsewhere the number will be found in the front of the local telephone directory.)
Breakdown 987
Auto-Moto Savez Jugoslavije (AMSJ) – Automobile Association of Yugoslavia.

DIRECTORY

Entertainment Information

The Calendar of Events in Yugoslavia, published annually, provides information for tourists. It can be obtained from all Yugoslav tourist offices and most large travel agencies. (See also **Special Events** page 105 and individual town/resort entries.)

Entry Formalities (see Arriving)

Health

Mains water is normally chlorinated, and while relatively safe may cause mild abdominal upsets. Bottled mineral water and excellent pure fruit juices are available. Milk is pasteurised and dairy products are safe for consumption, as are local meat, poultry, seafood, fruit and vegetables.

No vaccinations are required for entry into Yugoslavia.

Medical Care

Because of reciprocal arrangements, medical care is available in Yugoslavia when needed (with only a nominal charge for prescriptions, perhaps) for citizens of certain European countries including Britain. Citizens of most countries, including the US, Canada, Australia and New Zealand, must pay for any medical services, and though medical charges are very reasonable, some form of medical insurance is recommended. To receive treatment, British citizens need only produce their passport, or other travel document. All foreign visitors are automatically insured when using the country's public transport.

Emergency services are organised in most towns, including the resorts, and are ready to come to the aid of travellers and motorists using, if necessary, helicopters and motor launches at sea.

For Ambulance, in an emergency, dial 94. Otherwise, tour operators' representatives, hotel desks and tourist information offices can advise about hospitals and clinics. Treatment standards are adequate to excellent. 'Alternative' medicine, often with impressive modern facilities and success records, is widely on offer from Yugoslavia's numerous spa centres.

Spas

Yugoslavia has over 300 mineral and thermal springs.

There are over one hundred spas and rehabilitation and medical centres. The medical staff have knowledge and experience in using natural curative resources. In such centres each patient is approached individually and a programme is made according to his/her needs.

General Information:

Generalturist, 41000 Zagreb, Praška 4 (tel: (041) 420-888).

Holidays, Public

National (Federal) Holidays

New Year – 1 and 2 January; Labour Days – 1 and 2 May; Veteran's Day – 4 July; Republic Days – 29 and 30 November. If any of these holidays (except Veteran's Day) falls on a Sunday, the following Monday becomes a national holiday too.

DIRECTORY

Republican National Holidays
Each republic has its own 'Uprising Day'; some have additional holidays.:
Serbia – 7 July: Montenegro – 13 July: Slovenia – 27 April, 22 July and 1 November: Croatia – 27 July; Bosnia-Hercegovina – 27 July and 25 November; Macedonia – 2 August and 11 October.
NB. In Croatia and Slovenia, where the population is largely Roman Catholic, many people take holidays over Christmas and Easter.

Media

Press
The local national daily is *Borba*; it acts as the Communist Party voice. The English language daily is *Newsday*. The English-language *Yugoslav Life* is published monthly by the national news agency, but is rather 'heavy'. The leading papers of Europe and some overseas countries are available at newsagents, though they tend to appear only in larger coastal resorts and northern capitals. The press enjoys a great deal of freedom, and censorship is not imposed.

Radio
Radio Yugoslavia broadcasts daily news in English at 15.30, 18.30, 20.00 and 22.15 hours on short wave 31.9, 41.44 and 49.18 metres. Regional capitals also put out regular English-language bulletins (broadcasting frequencies and wavelengths can be found in the local press, or enquire at the tourist office).

Money Matters
The Yugoslav unit of currency is the dinar. A new dinar consisting of 100 paras was introduced on 1 January 1990, with the same value as 10,000 old dinars. From 1 January 1991, notes and coins in old dinar denominations are no longer valid.
Notes in circulation are to the value of 200, 100 and 50 dinars (with other denominations planned). Coins in circulation are to the value of 1 dinar and 50, 20 and 10 paras.
Lists of the current rates of exchange are always shown in a prominent place in exchange offices. Tourists can always obtain information about current rates of exchange from Yugoslav tourist representatives abroad. Travellers' cheques and foreign currency are accepted at banks, exchange offices and many hotels and official travel offices and some post offices. Keep all receipts. It is difficult to reconvert dinars into foreign currency.
Credit Cards: American Express, Access/Mastercard, Visa and Diners Club are readily accepted in hotels and major shops, etc.
Visitors' Tax: Tourists are charged this tax in resorts regardless of the kind of accommodation they use, including camping sites. Hotels and tourist offices collect the tax, which varies according to local regulations. During the off-season this tax is normally 50 per cent lower.

Opening Times
Shops: 08.00-12.00 hrs and 16.00-20.00 hrs Monday to Friday, and 08.00-15.00 hrs

DIRECTORY

Saturday (May to October) or 09.00-15.00 hrs Saturday (November to April). Many small, privately-owned shops are open late into the evening. Large department stores and self-service shops in major towns and tourist centres generally stay open throughout the day (08.00-20.00 hrs) Monday through Saturday and some self-service shops open on Sunday mornings, with some food-shops opening 06.00- 10.00 hrs. Most shops are closed on national and regional holidays (see **Holidays**).

Offices: 07.00-14.30 hrs Monday to Friday.

Government Offices: 07.00-15.00 hrs Monday to Friday.

Banks: Generally 07.30-15.00 hrs Monday to Friday. May close earlier or later, much depending on the size of the town.

Post offices: In major cities – 07.00-20.00 hrs Monday to Friday; elsewhere – 07.00-15.00 hrs or 08.00-12.00 and 17.00-19.00 hrs Monday to Friday. Most offices also open Saturday 07.00-15.00 hrs.

Museums and galleries: Varies. Most close on Monday, sometimes Sunday, and are generally open 09.00/10.00-12.00/13.00 hrs and some afternoons 16.00/17.00-18.00/19.00 hrs.

Comprehensive opening times for some of the larger museums appear in the main text.

Personal Safety

There are no undue dangers providing you do not go near, or take photographs of, military camps or installations (see also **Photography**).

Pharmacies

Well-supplied pharmacies or *Apoteka* (in Croatian, *Ljekarna*) are to be found in every major tourist centre, in all towns and larger settlements. In larger towns there is usually one open 24 hours. You will often find someone who speaks English.

Photography

Tourists may take photographs anywhere in Yugoslavia, except at certain military camps and installations and a few places such as railway stations and bridges that are clearly marked with the international sign (a camera with a cross through it). If caught, you may lose your film, and possibly your camera too.

Films made by the leading international producers (Kodak, Agfa, Fuji, etc) are on sale in the big towns.

Exposed film rolls can be developed and copied in several Yugoslav establishments with well-equipped photo laboratories, generally located in the large towns, and also in any of the numerous small-scale photographic shops in most towns. Tourists can send their films abroad for developing or take them with them, without restrictions or delay.

Places of Worship

Yugoslavia's mixture of Orthodox, Catholic and Muslim faiths provides a variety of places of worship. The Serbian Orthodox faith prevails in the republics of Serbia, Macedonia and Montenegro. Roman Catholicism predominates in Slovenia and Croatia, including Dalmatia. Bosnia divides itself

DIRECTORY

between Orthodox, Catholic and Muslim religions. Many Muslim communities also exist in Macedonia and southwest Serbia. Protestant churches are found in major towns and cities.

Police

Police are known as *Milicija* – stations are signposted and the national police emergency number is 92. The *milicija* are generally easygoing and helpful.

Post Office

Post offices *(pošta)* provide the usual services (see **Opening Times** for hours). Larger *pošta* have a poste restante desk; to claim your mail you will need your passport and have to pay a small fee. To send a letter poste restante, address it 'Poste Restante, Pošta' followed by the name of the town in Yugoslavia. To avoid long queues in post offices, stamps *(marka)* can be bought from kiosks. Airmail rates are liable to change; there is a lower rate for postcards.

Public Transport, internal

Air

The easiest method of overcoming long distances and the country's mountainous terrain is to fly. Yugoslavia's domestic air services provide connections between cities and towns along the coast and the interior of the country.
Main services are provided by the national carrier **JAT** (head office at Birčaninova 1/3, 11000 Beograd, tel: (011) 131-392 for domestic bookings), and **Adria Airways** (Kuzmičeva 7, 61000 Ljubljana, tel: (061) 313-366). JAT offer a wider choice of

Village church in Bled, Slovenia

destinations, flying to all 16 international airports and several smaller ones, while Adria Airways offer scheduled services between all major Yugoslav cities. In summer, additional services operate, especially to and from the Adriatic airports.
Domestic air travel represents good value, Yugoslavia has among the lowest fares in Europe – the cost of a flight is often little more than a standard rail fare for the same journey.

Rail

The rail system has, in recent years, been extended and modernised. There are good internal rail services based on a main line running from Ljubljana to Zagreb, Beograd and Skopje, with four branches to the coast. Overall, speeds are not high because of the nature of the terrain.
There are four types of train:

DIRECTORY

'ordinary' (stopping at all stations), 'fast', 'express', and 'rapide'. Travel is first or second class; most trains have a restaurant or buffet car, and night trains have sleeping cars or couchettes. To travel on express or rapide services a supplement is payable. Children under the age of four years travel free, those between four and 12 years receive a 50 per cent reduction, and students and young people in groups of six or more, a 30 per cent reduction on the fare.

The national timetable – *Vozni Red* – is available from bookshops and railway stations. You can purchase tickets in advance from authorised travel agents and so avoid queues at railway stations.

Bus

Cross-country. Bus services within the country are extremely well-developed. All tourist resorts can be reached by a regular and frequent service. Tourist centres and towns inland are linked by express buses, and during summer there are extra services.

Buses are cheaper and often faster than trains, although coastal services can be slow. You can usually pay on the bus, but not always, so whenever possible buy a ticket in advance.

Urban. There are good bus services in the main towns, with trams and trolleybuses in Beograd, and trams also in Zagreb and Sarajevo. Multiple-

Hydrofoils offer speed and comfort

DIRECTORY

journey tickets are sold through tobacconists. Fares paid to the driver are double the price of a pre-purchase ticket, which, incidentally, you are responsible for invalidating on board the bus, tram or trolleybus.

Taxi
Main cities and tourist resorts have a good metered taxi service – fairly inexpensive by European standards.

Sea Transport
The **Jadrolinija,** (Yugoslav Sea Traffic Company), Obala Jugoslovenske Mornarice 16, Rijeka (tel: (051) 22-356, and (051) 214-483) operates ships along the Adriatic coast and links the main tourist centres of Rijeka, Zadar, Split, Dubrovnik, as well as the smaller tourist resorts and numerous islands. Principal routes are Rijeka – Dubrovnik 'fast' service (24 hours), daily and Pula – Dubrovnik (via Rijeka and Split), weekly express.
Car ferries link up certain islands along the coast with the mainland.
Hydrofoil. Fast comfortable hydrofoils, based at larger towns on the Adriatic coast, maintain regular services to the most interesting places and islands along the coast. In the summer hydrofoils also run services to certain towns on the Italian coast.

Senior Citizens
Older and disabled visitors should be cautious in their choice of resorts and hotels as many are unsuitable for the less mobile. Where hotels are especially suitable, mention is made of this in the gazetteer. Yugoslavian transport and museums do not offer special concession to senior citizens.

Student and Youth Travel
There is a special organisation which deals with holidays and travel for young people and students in Yugoslavia.
Yugotours-Narom (The organisation for international and domestic youth travel), Djure Djakovića 31, 11000 Beograd (tel: (011) 764-622), has its own international Youth Centres in Dubrovnik, Rovinj, Bečići (near Budva) and Kopaonik, with suitable accommodation and entertainments for young people.
Yugotours-Narom specialises in the organisation of study and tourist trips throughout Yugoslavia, special interest programmes, accommodation, winter holidays, etc. To book, apply direct to Yugotours-Narom at the above address or to travel agencies who include these trips in their programme.

Telephones
Much of Yugoslavia's telephone system is fully automated, enabling callers to make direct-dial connections within the country, to most of Europe, and beyond.
When making a call, insert the coin(s) after lifting the receiver. The dialling tone (long and short tones) will then be heard. When making calls **within Yugoslavia,** precede the number with the relevant area code (shown in parentheses throughout this guide) unless calling locally.

DIRECTORY

Calls abroad can be made from certain payphones identified for international calls by having three or four coin slots for the higher denomination coins (or you can go to the post office and have your call placed for you). To call, first dial the international code (99 from Yugoslavia), followed by the country code (44 for the UK; 353 Eire; 1 the US and Canada), next the area code (minus the initial '0'), and lastly the subscriber's number. To dial Australia or New Zealand you have to go through the international operator (901). To dial **Yugoslavia from abroad,** use the international code (010 from the UK; 011 from the US and Canada), followed by the code for Yugoslavia (38), then the area code (minus the initial '0'), and finally the number.

Some Useful Numbers:
Operator 900
International Operator 901
Telephone Enquiries 988
General Information 9812

Time
Yugoslavia is one hour ahead of Greenwich Mean Time, and during summer two hours ahead, as clocks are forwarded by an hour in spring. For most of the year, therefore, Yugoslavia is one hour ahead of time in the United Kingdom, six hours ahead of American Eastern Standard Time, nine hours ahead of Pacific Standard Time, but nine hours behind eastern Australia and eleven hours behind New Zealand.

Tipping
Ten per cent is generally expected in hotels, restaurants and for taxis. There is usually a fixed charge for porters at airports, railway stations and quays.

Toilets
Public toilets sometimes have suspect plumbing and doors that do not lock, especially outside tourist areas. It is a good idea to carry a small amount of toilet paper, and tissues for drying your hands. On the whole, toilets in hotels, restaurants and larger department stores are modern and clean.

Tourist Offices

Abroad (Yugoslav National Tourist Office)
Great Britain: 143 Regent Street, London W1R 8AE (tel: (071) 734-5243 and (071) 439-0399).
US and Canada: 630 Fifth Avenue, Rockefeller Centre, Suite 280, New York, NY 10029 (tel: (212) 757-2801).

In Yugoslavia *(Turistički Informativni Centar)*
11000 **Beograd**: The subway at Ulica Terazije, next to the Albania Building, (tel: (011) 635-343 and (011) 635-622).
50000 **Dubrovnik**: Placa 1 (tel: (050) 26-354 and (050) 26-355).
61000 **Ljubljana**: Titova 11 (tel: (061) 224-222 and (061) 215-412).
21000 **Novi Sad**: Dunavska 27 (tel: (021) 51-888).
52000 **Pula**: Trg Bratstva i Jedinstva 4 (tel: (052) 34-355).
51000 **Rijeka**: Trg Republike 9 (tel: (051) 33-909).
71000 **Sarajevo**: JNA 50 (tel: (071) 25-151).
91000 **Skopje**: Stokovna Kuća Most, Skopska Čaršija (tel: (091) 223-429).

DIRECTORY

58000 **Split**: Titova Obala 12 (tel: (058) 42-142).
41000 **Zagreb**: Trg Nikole Zrinjskog 14: (tel: (041) 411-883). In addition to the above centres there are local information offices (Turistički Biro) in nearly all tourist resorts in Yugoslavia, to which you can go for reservation of accommodation in private homes. You may address your correspondence to the Turistički Biro of the place you wish to visit. (See also individual gazetteer entries for some other tourist information addresses.)

Travel Agencies

Below is a list of useful agencies to be found in some of the main towns and resorts. They can provide tickets for domestic and external travel, sightseeing excursions, or hunting/fishing trips.

Atlas, Pile 1, 50000 Dubrovnik (tel: (050) 27-333 and (050) 22-222).
Autotehna – Avis, Bulevar Revolucije 94, 11000 **Beograd** (tel: (011) 433-323 and (011) 433-314).
Dalmacijaturist, Titova Obala 5, 58000 **Split** (tel: (058) 44-666 and (058) 45-643).
Emona Globtour, Šmartinska 130/x, 561000 **Ljubljana** (tel: (061) 444-177).
Generalturist, Praška 5, 41000 **Zagreb** (tel: (041) 420-888).
Ina Tours, Savska Cesta 41, POB 333, 41000 **Zagreb** (tel: (041) 535-316 and (041) 535-318).
Inex Turist, Trg Republike 5, 11000 **Beograd** (tel: (011) 622-360 and (011) 629-322).
Interimpex, Veljko Vlahović 10, 91000 **Skopje** (tel: (091) 228-644

National costume, southern Croatia

and (091) 228-572).
Kompas Jugoslavija, Pražakova 4, 61000 **Ljubljana** (tel: (061) 327-761 and (061) 327-661).
Kvarner-Express, Maršala Tita 186 and 192, 51410 **Opatija** (tel: (051) 711-111).
HTO Montenegroturist, Oour Montenegro-Express, Trg Edvarda Kardelja 2, 81310 **Budva** (tel: (086) 41-116).
Olimpik-Turs, Brankova 21, 71000 **Sarajevo** (tel: (071) 24-328).
Putnik, Dragoslava Jovanovića 1, 11000 **Beograd** (tel: (011) 332-591-6).
Srbija-Turist, Voždova 12, 18000 **Niš** (tel: (018) 25-047, (018) 25-249 and (018) 25-126).
Unis-Turist, Tršćanska 7, 71000 **Sarajevo** (tel: (071) 202-070).
Vojvodinatours, Bulevar Maršala Tita 19, 21000 **Novi Sad** (tel: (021) 616-322 and (021) 615-703).
Yugotours, Djure Djakovića 31, 11000 **Beograd** (tel: (011) 764-622).

LANGUAGE

The principal language in Yugoslavia is Serbo-Croat, broadly speaking written in the Latin alphabet in the north and west, and in the Cyrillic alphabet in the east and south, though main signs in Cyrillic areas are often given in both alphabets.

A	L
B	Lj
C	M
Ć	N
Č	Nj
D	O
Dz	P
D (Dj)	R
E	S
F	Š
G	T
H	U
I	V
J	Z
K	Ž

Slovenian and Macedonian are substantially different but all are pronounced phonetically, so it is useful to know the following rules of pronunciation:
a as in father
c = ts as in cats
ć = ch as in chair
č = tch as in batch
e as in net
i as in if
j = y as in yet
o as in not
š = sh as in shack
u as in put
ž = zh as in treasure

English is widely spoken in tourist areas and increasingly elsewhere, especially by the young. But any effort made by foreigners to speak a few words in Serbo-Croat gives great pleasure.

Essentials
yes da
no ne
please molim vas
yes please da, molim vas
no thank you ne, hvala
thank you hvala

Questions and Requests
where is/are...? gde je/su...?
when? kada?
how much is/are...? šta košta/koštaju...?
how far? koliko je daleko?
what's that? šta je to?
what do you want? šta želite?
what must I do? šta treba da radim?
have you...? imate li...?
is there...? ima li...?
have you seen...? jeste li videli...?
may I have...? mogu li...?
I want/should like... hteo bih/želeo bih...
I don't want... ne želim...

Useful Statements
here is/are... evo...
I like it svidja mi se
I don't like it ne svidja mi se
I know znam
I don't know ne znam
I think so mislim
I'm hungry gladan sam
I'm thirsty žedan sam
I'm tired umoran sam
I'm in a hurry žurim
I'm ready gotov sam
leave me alone pustite me na miru
just a moment trenutak
it's cheap nije skupo
it's too expensive suviše je skupo

Language Problems
do you speak English? govorite li engleski?
I don't speak Serbo-Croat ne govorim srpskohrvatski

LANGUAGE

I don't understand ne razumem
would you say that again, please? da li biste bili ljubazni da ponovite?
please speak slowly molim vas, govorite polako

Polite Phrases/Greetings

sorry/excuse me izvinite/oprostite
not at all/don't mention it nema na čemu
it doesn't matter nije važno
I beg your pardon? What? šta ste rekli?
good/that's fine dobro/odlično
good morning dobro jutro
good day/good afternoon dobar dan
good evening dobro veče
good night laku noć
how are you? kako ste?
very well, thank you hvala, dobro
goodbye dovidjenja
where are you from? odakle ste?
may I introduce you to my wife/husband? Mogu li da vam predstavim svoga ženu/muža?
cheers! živeli!

Money and Travel

Is there an exchange bureau near here? ima li neka menjačnica u blizini?
do you cash travellers' cheques? menjate li travellers čekove?
Customs Carina
Passport control Pašoska kontrola
your passport please vaš pasoš, molim
have you anything to declare? imate li nešto da prijavite?
this is my luggage ovo je moj prtljag
a second class ticket to... kartu druge kalse/drugog razreda do...
a return to... jednu povratnu kartu za...
where can I buy air tickets? gde mogu da kupim avionske karte?

is there a flight to London on Thursday? leti li avion za London četvrtkom?
when does it leave/arrive? kada polazi/dolazi?
when is the next plane? kada leti sledeći avion?
when must I check in? kada treba da dam na aerodromu?
where can I rent a car? gde mogu da iznajmim kola?
I want to rent a car and a driver/a self-drive car hteo bih da iznajmimkola sa šoferom/bez šofera
where is a car park? gde je parking?
where is the nearest petrol station? gde je najbliza benzinska pumpa?

Accommodation

have you a room for the night? imate li jednu sobu za jednu noć?
I'd like a room with a balcony želeo bih sobu sa balkonom
how much is the room per night? šta košta soba?
how much is the room without meals? koliko košta samo soba, bez pansiona?
where's the bathroom? gde je kupatilo?
where's the lavatory? gde je klozet/zahod?
is there a shower? ima li duš?
key to room number 315 please tri stotine petnaest, molim
where is the dining room? gde je trpezarija?
I need a guide/interpreter potreban mi je vodič/tumač
are there any letters for me? ima li pošte za mene?
can you have my bill ready? možete li mi spremiti račun?
thank you for a pleasant stay hvala, bilo je vrlo prijatno

LANGUAGE

In the Restaurant
beer pivo
bill račun
bread hleb/kruh
butter buter
cheese sir
coffee kafa
cup šolja/šalica
fork viljuška/vilica
glass čaša
knife nož
menu jelovnik
milk mleko
pepper biber/papar
plate tanjur
salt so
spoon kašika/žlica
sugar šećer
table sto
tea čaj
vegetarian vegetarijanski
vinegar sirće/ocat
waiter konabar
waitress konabarica
water voda
wine vino
wine list vinska karta

On the Menu
hors d'oeuvres predjela
soups supa/čorbe/juhe
fish ribe
meat meso
grills roštilj
poultry and game živina i divljač
vegetables and salads povrće (varivo) i salate
eggs jaja
dessert kolači (desert)
fruit voće
drinks pića

Days of the week
Monday Ponedeljak
Tuesday Utorak
Wednesday Sreda
Thursday Četvrtak
Friday Petak
Saturday Subota
Sunday Nedelja

Months of the year
January Siječanj
February Veljača
March Ožujak
April Travanj
May Svibanj
June Lipanj
July Srpanj
August Kolovoz
September Rujan
October Listopad
November Studeni
December Prosinac

Numbers
0 nula
1 jedan
2 dva
3 tri
4 četiri
5 pet
6 šest
7 sedam
8 osam
9 devet
10 deset
11 jedanaest
12 dvanaest
13 trinaest
14 četrnaest
15 petnaest
16 šesnaest
17 sedamnaest
18 osamnaest
19 devetnaest
20 dvadeset
21 dvadeset jedan
30 trideset
40 četrdeset
50 pedeset
60 šezdeset
70 sedamdeset
80 osamdeset
90 devedeset
100 sto
200 dvesta
300 trista
400 četiri stotine
1,000 hiljadu

INDEX

accommodation (see also regional details) 99-100
air travel 109-10, 119
Ankaran 41
Avala 15

Bajrakli Džamija 12
Banja Luka 18
Bar 64
Bečići 33
Belgrade see Beograd
Beograd 11-17
Biograd 29
Biševo 65
Bitola 77
Blagaj 25
Bled 67-8
Bohinjsko Jezero 68-9
Boka Kotorska 30-2
Bovec 69
Brač 32-3
Brijuni Islands 55
budget tips 104-5
Budva 33
buses 120-1

camping 112
car rental 115
Cavtat 34
Cetinje 77-8
children's entertainment 104
climate 101-2
Cres-Lošinj 35-6
Crikvenica 36
culture, entertainment and nightlife (see also regional details) 100-1
currency 112, 117
customs regulations 112

Djerdap Gorge 19-20
Dojransko Ezero 78
driving 112-15
Dubrovnik 37-9
Durmitor Sinjavina 79-80, 96

eating out (see also regional details) 97-8
Elafiti Islands 40

embassies and consulates 115
emergencies 115-16
entry formalities 109

ferries 111, 121
festivals and events 105-6
food and drink 97-8
Fruška Gora 20-1, 26

Galerija Fresaka (Beograd) 12
Golubački Grad 19, 20

Heraclea Lyncestis 77
Hercegnovi 30-1
history of Yugoslavia 7, 10
Hvar 6, 40, 41

Iron Gate Gorge see Djerdap Gorge
Izola 40-1

Jajce 21-2
Josip Brož Tito Spomenik 12-13

Kalemegdan 13-14
Kanjiža Spa 17-18
Kobarid 69
Koločep 40
Komiža 65
Konak Kneginje Ljubice 14
Kopaonik 80
Koper 41
Korčula 42-3, 111
Kotor 29, 32
Kranjska Gora 5, 69-70
Krk 43
Krusedol 21

Lepenski Vir 20
Lipica 70-1
Ljubljana 71-2
local etiquette 102-3
local time 122
Lopud 40
Lovran 43
Lumbarda 42
Lun 55

Makarska 44-5

maps
  Beograd 16-17
  Dalmatia 44-5
  Dubrovnik Old Town 37
  Eastern Europe 4
  Istria and the Kvarner 50-1
  Southern Adriatic Coast 30-1
  Yugoslavia 8-9
  Zagreb 74-5
media 117
medical treatment 116
Medjugorje 23
Miločer 61-2
Mlini 35
Mljet 46, 92-3
money 112, 117
Mostar 23-5
Motovun 65
Muzej Savremene Umetnosti (Beograd) 14

Narodni Muzej (Beograd) 14
national parks and reserves 90-6
naturism 103-4
Niš 80-1
Novi Pazar 81
Novi Sad 25-6
Novigrad 46
Novo Hopovo 21

Ohrid 82-3
Ohridsko Ezero 82, 90
Omiš 47
Opatija 47-8
opening times 117-18
Orebić 48

Pag 55
passports and visas 109
Peć 83-4
Perast 31-2
personal safety 103, 118
Petrovac 62
Petrovaradin Fortress 24, 25
pharmacies 118
photography 118
Piran 49

127

INDEX

places of worship 118-19
Plat 35
Plitvička Jezera 72, 91-2
Podgora 45-6
police 119
Poreč 49, 52
Portorož 52
post offices 119
Postojnska Jama 73, 96
Prčanj 32
Prejkamski Grad 73
Prepansko Ezero 84, 90
Primošten 53
Prizren 84-5
public holidays 116-17
public transport 119-21
Pula 53-5

Rab 55
Rabac 55-6
rail travel 110, 119-20
Rijeka 56-7
Risan 31
Rovinj 57

Sarajevo 26-8
Selce 36
senior citizens 121

shopping (*see also* regional details) 98-9
Šibenik 58
Šipan 40
Skadarlija 14-15
Skadarsko Jezero 85-6, 90
Škocjanske Jame 74-5
Skopje 86
Slano 58
Smederevo 19
spas 116
Split 59-60
sport and leisure facilities 28, 68-70, 80, 106-8
Srebreno 35
Sremski Karlovci 26
Ston 49
Studenica 81
student and youth travel 121
Suka Punta 55
Sutomore 64
Sveti Stefan 61

taxis 121
telephones 121-2
tipping 122
Tito's Mausoleum 13

Tivat 32
toiletries 103
toilets 122
tourist offices 122-3
travel agencies 123
travel to Yugoslavia 109-11
Trogir 62-3
Trsteno 59
Tučepi 45

Ulcinj 63
Umag 64-5

Vis 65
visitors' tax 117
voltage 115
Vrdnik 21
Vrsar 66

wildlife and countryside 87-96
winter sports 28, 68-70, 80
words and phrases 124-6

Žabljak 79
Zadar 66
Zagreb 75-6

The Automobile Association would like to thank the following photographers and libraries for their assistance in the preparation of this book:

INTERNATIONAL PHOTOBANK
Cover Old Bridge at Mostar, 5 Kranjska Gora, 6 Hvar, 7 Musician, 21 Waterfall Jajce, 23 Souvenir shop, 27 Trad. folk dance, 34 Cavtat, 38 Dubrovnik, 39 Dubrovnik fountain, 41 Hvar, 47 Opatija, 49 Piran, 53 Pula, 54 Rab, 56 Rabac, 59 Split, 61 Hotel Sveti Stefan, 62 Trogir cathedral, 67 L Bled, 68 L Bohinj, 70 Kranjska Gora, 73 Waterfalls Plitvice, 87 L Bohinj, 97 Korčula Market, 99 Hotel Liburna, 100 Folk dancers, 105 Hvar Nat. Folk Ensemble, 109 Hydrofoil, 113 Mt. Triglav, 119 Bled, 120 Hydrofoil, 123 Folk costume.

NATURE PHOTOGRAPHERS LTD 88 Cliffs Montenegro (E A Janes), 89 Southern festoon, 95 Peach-leaved bellflower (P R Sterry).

SPECTRUM COLOUR LIBRARY 24 Novi Sad, 29 Kotor, 33 Budva, 42 Korčula, 44 Makarska, 64 Ulcinj fish-traps, 83 Ohrid market, 90 L Ohrid, 98 Ulcinj market, 107 Windsurfing, 111 Ship, 114 Julian Alps.

YUGOSLAVIA TOURIST BOARD 11 Beograd Nat. Museum, 13 Kalemegdan fortress, 19 Golubački Grad, 22 Medjugorje, 77 Heraclea Lyncestis mosaic, 78 L Dojran, 79 Zabljak, 80 Kopaonik, 81 Wall painting, 85 L Skadar, 92 Plitvice Lakes Nat. Park.